DADDY

DADDY

The Diary of an Expectant Father

Dennis Danziger

The Body Press
Tucson, Arizona

TO MY PARENTS

The Body Press
A division of HPBooks, Inc.
575 East River Road
Tucson, Arizona 85704

Manufactured in the United States of America

10 9 8 7 6 5 4 3 2 1

First Edition

Library of Congress Cataloging-in-Publication Data

Danziger, Dennis, 1951-
    Daddy : the diary of an expectant father.

    1. Danziger, Dennis, 1951- . 2. Fathers—
United States—Diaries.   I. Title
HQ756.D35A   1987   306.8'742'0924   86-71873

ISBN 0-89586-526-2

ACKNOWLEDGEMENT

It takes more people to produce a book than it does to produce a baby. I have been fortunate to have had wonderful partners in both undertakings.

When I was a student at the University of Texas, I had a notion that I wanted to be a writer, but had no idea how to go about it. One of the best things that ever happened to me was the morning I wandered into a creative writing class taught by the novelist and non-fiction writer, Michael Mewshaw. Michael encouraged me, advised me, beat me at tennis and published my first short story. He helped make me a writer. I have no idea how to adequately thank him for that.

Fifteen years later and several thousand miles apart (he is a professor of literature at the American Academy in Rome), I sent Michael the first few pages of DADDY. He thought I was onto something and encouraged me to keep at it. From Los Angeles to Rome and back, my pages traveled and always they returned with suggestions that improved my work.

ACKNOWLEDGEMENT

For his friendship and advice, I am grateful.

I am also grateful to my friends, Sybil Adelman, Martin Sage, and Arlene Weiss, who introduced me to my agent, Charlotte Sheedy, who told me "don't worry, I'll sell the book." And she did. In addition to her editorial skills, Charlotte's wisdom and her cool voice of reason (transmitted by phone from the opposite coast) have comforted me in moments of mild hysteria.

"This is Sam Mitnick from HP BOOKS. And I want to publish DADDY," is without a doubt the most magical message anyone has ever left on my telephone answering machine. It has unfortunately been erased, but it is a line I will never forget. I thank Sam for taking a chance on this first time author. And I hope the upshot from this book, if any, makes him look good for having taken the risk.

Melodee Spevack, Rachel Travers and Sue Bugden helped me in the preparation of this manuscript. Gregory McNamee was instrumental in bringing my work to my publisher's attention. Vicky Bijur, Charlotte's associate, kept me informed of the day-to-day progress as related to this book. It was always a pleasure hearing from her. My friend and lawyer, Robert Brenner, explained to me what I was agreeing to by signing my contract. Bob's sense of humor (which he shares, without running the clock) made all that legalese a lot less intimidating.

I have a deep prejudice toward the entire staff of The Women's Medical Group of Santa Monica. I love them. Throughout the pregnancy, they treated my wife, Ellen Sandler, as well as myself, with sensitivity and kindness. They, Drs. Karen Blanchard, Marki Knox, Katie Moyer, James Gordon, Patricia Robertson and Roz Warner and Jacqueline Snow MN, NP, kept us informed, they respected

ACKNOWLEDGEMENT

our needs and wishes, they listened. Their care and concern made us able to relax and enjoy this special time.

Shortly after our child was born, we were blessed again. Zhang Xuesu, a graduate student from China, who is studying early childhood development in America, helped take care of our baby. Su, a mother of a fivefour year old boy, was vastly more experienced at parenting than we were. She not only taught us, but she became a third parent to our child. The sweetness of our child's spirit is certainly due in part to the tenderness and love she showed him.

As new parents we were also fortunate to meet and study with Magda Gerber and the staff of the Resources for Infant Educaters in LA whose simple and wise philosophy of respect for the child and awareness of the child's point of view has proven to be the best childrearing education we could have possibly received.

Drs. Marshall Sachs, John Tarle, Dennis Woo and Robert Hamilton of the Santa Monica Pediatric Medical Group provided excellent health care for our newborn and soothed us even during those frantic middle of the night calls when we were certain our child's diaper rash required immediate medical attention.

Finally, I would like to thank my wife, writer-director, Ellen Sandler. For ten years, Ellen and I have worked together as a team in the theatre, in television and in film. But by far the greatest of our many creations are our children. Unlike our previous collaborations in which we try to split the work 50-50, this time Ellen literally carried the full weight. She did so with diginity and with love. So much so that I was able to shed some of my fear of pregnancy and babies and to experience even before our child's birth the joy of impending fatherhood.

ACKNOWLEDGEMENT

As always, Ellen was the first person to read my work, to comment upon it and to send me back to my desk for revisions. There were times when her criticisms were painful to hear, particularly when she was right, but in the long run, these observations vastly improved the pages you are about to read.

D.J.D.
July 22, 1986
Los Angeles, CA

CONTENTS

CONTENTS

DADDY

I
SEX WITHOUT
CONTRACEPTIVES

December 5, 1983

It was the second night of our honeymoon, and we were both eager to consummate our marriage.

"You want to make a baby?" Ellen asked.

"I'd love to make a baby. I'm just not sure I want to make a teenager."

This conversation took place in bed at the Glenborough Inn in Santa Barbara, California, about thirty hours after we had been married in Los Angeles, which is where we live.

I suppose it is odd not to consummate one's marriage as quickly as possible, but we were exhausted on our wedding night from eating, dancing, and from the drive up.

Besides, it wasn't like we were the blushing bride and groom. We had consummated our friendship on July 4, 1976, after witnessing Jerry Koosman one-hit the Chicago Cubs in Shea Stadium. We are hardly in our rookie year.

I'm thirty-two. And a half. Ellen's a few years older. Babywise, the clock is ticking. If we are to have a family, we've got to get started.

Call me old-fashioned, but the one aspect of fatherhood I insisted upon was that before we had a child, before we even conceived one, we'd be married. I don't think kids are as liberal as everyone thinks. Given the choice, which no kid ever is, he'd rather be legitimate.

Until yesterday, bringing a child into our lives was purely theoretical. For months, even years, when Ellen and I discussed parenthood, we both expressed ambivalence. There were financial considerations, career considerations, and even a troubling question that Ellen brought up for the first time as we lay in each other's arms in a Santa Barbara inn.

"You know, there is the possibility that we can't have a child."

"Rubbish," I said. "If we make love without contraceptives, we'll have a kid. First time, every time. Believe me, it'll go like clockwork. Make love, get a baby. No question in my mind."

"It doesn't necessarily work that way. What if you have a low sperm count?"

"My sperm count is so high, it's practically off the chart!"

"When did you ever have a sperm count?"

"Ellen, I am not going to lie here on my honeymoon night and discuss my sperm count. People have questioned my sanity. People have questioned my integrity. But no one has ever questioned my sperm count."

We held each other and reminisced about our wedding. We had written our own vows. We had promised to share the responsibilities of marriage, to stand beside each other in times of uncertainty and fear, to appreciate the commonplace and the everyday pleasures. We promised to make each other laugh. We have been doing that for a long time. But there will come a day maybe thirty years from now, maybe thirty days from now, when one of us would die, when one of us would be left alone. We talked about that day, we held each other, we cried. Then we tried to make a baby.

December 6, 1983

It was just after midnight when our marriage was consummated. Ellen scrunched up her face, put her hand to her temple.

"There's a throbbing in my head," she said. "You're going to think I'm crazy, but I really believe I'm pregnant."

"Of course you're pregnant. You married a man, not a field mouse. Now let's see, today's December 6th, our child should be born right about the time the pennant races heat up. We'll think of a name in the morning. Good night."

December 7, 1983

After her morning shower, Ellen emerged from the bathroom and announced that she was definitely not pregnant. The throbbing in her head, she theorized, was one too many glasses of wine at dinner.

I pulled the covers over my head and began worrying about my sperm count.

December 8, 1983

As we drove back to Los Angeles, Ellen and I began to think of the many things we were eager to teach our child.

"Gourmet cooking is something every child needs to learn," Ellen said.

"At a very early age," I added. "By eight or nine at the latest, a child should have mastered desserts. Chocolate mousse, truffles, fresh fruit tarts, hazelnut cake."

"Cleaning is another area in which children love to excel," Ellen said. "There is nothing that makes a boy or girl happier than the sight of a well-vacuumed den."

"I remember how delighted I was on my fourth birthday when my mother let me scrub the oven all by myself. To become a useful member of the household is so essential in a child's development."

"And then there's ironing."

"And don't forget lawn mowing, A great ego booster."

"And doing dishes. Lots and lots of dishes."

December 12, 1983

Ellen convinced me that we should apply for a loan in order to build up a substantial amount of credit so that one day, if we're lucky, we'll be able to take an even bigger loan in order to make a down payment on a home and then be strapped with a mortgage for the rest of our lives. Thus, nine days after I said "I do," I am voluntarily digging my way into debt. With a much larger debt in the foreseeable future. So this is married life.

December 29, 1983

"Do my breasts look bigger this morning?"

"Bigger than what?" I asked.

"Bigger than yesterday. Bigger than last week. Bigger than when we first met."

Our relationship is changing. The traditional opening line, "What do you want for breakfast?" has been replaced by "Do my breasts look any bigger?"

Thus, I suppose, the evolution from childlessness to parenthood begins.

December 31, 1983

New Year's Eve in New York City. I can hear the firecrackers exploding down the street. The drunks' booming voices. The music and happy feet pound through the ceiling.

New Year's Eve. The liquor stores are still open and crammed with customers. Everyone everywhere is getting juiced.

I've had a few glasses of wine, too. Maybe I want to forget a lot of this past year. Maybe I'm glad it's over. Maybe it's too scary to think about the coming year. The coming week.

By the time Ellen and I go to bed this evening, we will both be sober. We will continue into 1984 what we began late in 1983. We have already labeled 1984 "The Year of Pregnancy." We have no idea what fate will bring us in the coming year, but of those events that we have some control over, we hope '84 brings us a child.

January 2, 1984

The Year of Pregnancy was hit with a five yard loss this morning when Ellen reported exactly four weeks to the day since we undertook this project that she was definitely not pregnant . . . again.

Having put a great deal of time, energy and imagination into this project, we find ourselves having to step up the pace. Though we have been eager collaborators in the first month, we sometimes shucked our duty: staying out far into the night and dragging home exhausted, bloated and more in the mood for sleep than love.

Due to our lack of discipline in the first month, we have agreed by a vote of 2-0 to initiate what is referred to in the world of sports as two-a-days. A morning workout, followed by a late afternoon or early evening scrimmage, will commence tomorrow at 0800 hours. In addition, there will be no days off. Partying will be kept to a minimum. Food and drink intake will be moderate. Eight hours of sleep a night is mandatory. And, of course, there will be constant bed checks.

If a month from now we have fulfilled all our requirements and we remain empty-handed (or empty-bellied), we may consult a professional.

January 10, 1984

Ellen consulted a professional. I encouraged this session assuming the good doctor would confirm the wisdom of my procreative plan. She did not.

Under normal circumstances, patients take their doctor's advice. But when a woman trying to become pregnant walks into her gynecologist's office and the doctor is eight months' pregnant, as Dr. Lowell is, there can be no doubt that the patient will carry out the doctor's orders.

Unfortunately, the first thing Dr. Vicky Lowell did was to chuck my sensible "two-a-day" plan, replacing it with a cruel "once-every-other-day" plan. If one is trying to impregnate his wife, the logical thing to do is have intercourse. But, according to Dr. Lowell, the best way for Ellen to get pregnant is NOT to have intercourse. At least, not to have intercourse more than once every forty-eight hours.

Dr. Lowell's plan seems foolish. But I'd feel more foolish not taking the doctor's advice after Ellen paid her a hundred dollars for a twenty-minute visit. So, now it's every other night. Which I can live with. What I can't live with is the explanation. I'm not sure of the medical terminology, but the reason for this unnecessary restraint has something to do with giving my sperm a chance to build up, gather fellow sperm and become strong. It's as if my sperm is pumping iron. All of this is absurd. My sperm is built up and strong and ready to go whenever needed. Always has been, always will be.

I am told that if, after three months, Ellen's still not pregnant, I'll have to submit to a sperm count.

Well, there's no way I am submitting to a sperm count. It's degrading. To take a sperm count, Ellen and I would go to bed. So far, so good. But then as I become sexually aroused and near my climactic moment, I'd have to excuse myself, race to the bathroom and make love to a mustard jar.

No, thank you.

Suddenly, making babies, like everything else in the modern world, is in the hands of a specialist. Such nonsense. When my grandparents were fleeing Russia and walking across Europe toward America, did my grandfather stop and say:

"Mollie, what say we go to Prague and see a fertility specialist?"

My grandfather, may he rest in peace, said:

"Bubbee, we've got five strong boys. Why don't we make a little girl to help with the dishes?"

And that night they made Aunt Jenny.

In 1984, with five billion people crowding the planet, we in middle-class America pay a professional to tell us what every junior high school kid already knows. If you want to make a baby, you've just got to do it.

January 14, 1984

I was at a photography museum this afternoon where I picked up a photo album called "Giving Birth." There were pictures of nine-months' pregnant women posing nude with their husbands or children. Pregnant women in their nightgowns, pregnant women holding pregnant rabbits. All very cute. Very "Isn't life beautiful?"

Then I turned the page and saw a bloodied baby's head squeezing out from between the legs of his terrified mother. A picture of a blood-slicked baby the moment he was completely free of his mother's body. A picture of a doctor clipping the umbilical cord.

The more pages I turned, the more graphically medical the book became. The more explicit the pictures, the weaker I became.

"Look at the horror in their faces," Ellen said, pointing to a mother observing the delivery of her child.

"They should be on drugs!" I snapped.

"You know, you're going to have to be in the delivery room with me. You know I'm not going to go in that delivery room alone," she said.

"Of course you won't be alone. There'll be a doctor, nurses. Maybe my mother will show up."

"You'll be there. Helping! You still think you want a child?"

I think I do. In my mind, the kid's 18 months old and we're chatting about Sesame Street and licking popsicles and having a great time.

The blood, the pain and the medical expenses haven't yet become real to me. But I've got a feeling I can't avoid them too much longer.

January 15, 1984

Ever since Dr. Lowell put us on the "Alternating Fornicating" system, Ellen and I have performed like clockwork. Once every 48 hours.

One thing is certain, every other night I have no trouble falling asleep. Tonight, however, Ellen voiced a complaint.

"It's just so unromantic knowing that Tuesday, Thursday and Saturday are our days of the week."

"But, the following week, we switch to Monday, Wednesday, Friday. Kind of keeps us on our toes, doesn't it?"

"Sex has become routine. Suddenly it's like a homework assignment, knowing what to expect on what nights."

"Hey! Don't look at me! You're the one who wanted this woman gynecologist. I'm sure we can find plenty of men ob/gyns who'll tell you to do it whenever you can. On subways, in the back of taxis, anywhere, anytime."

"I just don't feel excited about it anymore. There's no anticipation, no suspense anymore. I no longer think, 'Should I dab on some perfume and arouse him, or should we opt for the crossword puzzle?'"

"Leave the crossword puzzle alone. We're on tonight."

"That's exactly what I mean. 'We're on.' I feel like a baby-making machine. Can't you at least try to create a mood?"

"How about if I take you out for a pizza and when we come back we'll do it on the living room floor?"

She made a noise. It sounded like "uhhhch." It's the noise women make to express their thorough disgust of men. A disgust so deep that no word can convey the depth of its passion.

But in time, the anger and accusations subside. The crossword puzzle is brought to bed, but all its squares are left unmarked and we lapse back into our glorious routine.

January 17, 1984

Tonight we came home late, cold and tired. It is Thursday. A scheduled stop on the road to parenthood. We are both exhausted. With each other's consent, we ignore our obligation. I go to sleep fearing an early morning call from Dr. Lowell.

"Did you do what you were supposed to do last night?" Dr. Lowell asks.

"Actually, the theatre let out late and we had trouble catching a cab."

"When you're old and childless in Miami Beach and other people are getting birthday cards from their grandchildren, and all you're getting is social security checks, don't blame me!"

As I start to hang up on Dr. Lowell, I hear:

"And doing it twice tomorrow night doesn't make up for today. It's like missing a night's sleep. Once you miss you can never catch up!"

January 20, 1984

Imagine W.C. Fields' nose if it had a two-thousand-a-week cocaine habit. That's what my schnozz looks like. My ears feel as if they've been trapped on an elevator stuck between the 81st and 82nd floors. And there is an annoying little man inside my head playing round after round of darts against the backs of my eyeballs. Welcome to my all-night, cross-country, three-takeoff-with-one-unscheduled-landing airplane headache.

All of this misery could be extinguished as quickly as it takes one to throw back one's head and swallow. But no! I cannot have my aspirin unless I want to really suffer. Suffer the headache that lingers for an eternity—marital guilt.

Once upon a time, Ellen read that aspirin breaks down one's chromosomes. She has concluded, without one shred of scientific evidence, that it would be unsafe for either of us to take aspirin while we're trying to reproduce. Since she is not the one with the headache, she has no trouble enforcing the "no aspirin" law as if it were a capital offense.

"Go on, take three, four aspirin," she'd say. "Swallow the whole damn bottle. And when our child comes out looking like Flipper, we'll know whose fault it is."

My headache endures. The sacrifices this would-be parent suffers without even knowing for certain whether his child has been conceived continue to mount.

Ever so slowly, one small step at a time, the focus of my life shifts. Numero Uno is not Numero Uno anymore.

January 28, 1984

In the middle of this smoggy L.A. afternoon, without having done anything constructive from the time we got up, we went back to bed and made love. Sometime afterwards, Ellen recorded an "x" on the appropriate line of the temperature/love-making chart she must send to Dr. Lowell at the end of the month. This daily temperature taking has something to do, though I'm not sure what, with ovulation and babymaking.

Several hours later, Ellen told me that she started having her period. We both lapsed into immediate depression. In the past two months we've been going at it like a couple of college freshmen in love and unchaperoned for the first time. But two months of trying, and nothing. Ellen's immediate thought is that it's too late. We talked about it for years. She wavered. I was adamantly opposed. I was too young. I wasn't ready. I was financially unstable. I was scared. Now we're scared that it won't happen. That we'll never have a baby. That's a problem we can't go back and fix.

February 11, 1984

Late this evening I rushed Ellen home from a party. She was feeling nauseated. In the car she was doubled up, clutching her stomach and moaning the entire 8.4 miles home.

"Could this be the much-talked-about morning sickness?" she asked.

"How could it be? It's after midnight," I said.

"It doesn't necessarily come in the morning. You can get morning sickness anytime."

"Oh."

"You mean you didn't know that?"

"Men don't necessarily know these things."

"Men don't know a lot of things," she said.

"And women don't know who won the Cy Young Award in 1967. So there."

I raced home, taking all the shortcuts I knew. Whenever I made conversation to try to take her mind off her pain, she told me not to bother. That she was too weak to think about talking. Just before we got home, she said:

"I always thought I would be immune to morning sickness. I don't know why. I thought since I'm in such good health, I wouldn't get nauseous. Of course, this may not be morning sickness. It could just be something I ate, or it could be menstrual cramps, or it could be from over-exercising today. It could be anything."

I pulled up in front of our house, flipped Ellen the keys and watched her spring up the sidewalk into the house. As the house lights came on, I had a strange thought. I was rooting for my wife to have morning sickness, and hoping she would have it again and again and again.

February 13, 1984

This morning's breakfast conversation was limited to the reasons we would not make good parents. I'd worry too much and make the child paranoid. Ellen would demand too much and make the child neurotic. I would stress sports too heavily and make the child a jock. Or worse, a frustrated and a failed jock.

We went on and on discussing our shortcomings, figuring out in what ways the child would turn out to be a mess.

"Little Harold will be forty-three years old and still dependent on us. Kiss the Golden Years goodbye."

"Maybe this is God's way of telling us we shouldn't have a baby."

"Maybe."

We are already preparing ourselves for the possibility of being a childless couple. We know our excuses are just that—excuses to prepare us for such a letdown. We also know that in our hearts, that more than anything else, we want a baby.

February 23, 1984

As of today, we are 0-for-3 months, depressed, confused, possibly running out of time or indeed, out of time and out of the ballgame.

"I don't want to go to another doctor and shell out a ton of money," Ellen said. "After all, I gave Dr. Lowell $100 and what did I get for it? A thermometer."

So, we are switching game plans. Having failed at the "everyday," "two-a-day" and "every-other-day" routines, we are going into a new phase. The semi-Orthodox Jewish method.

Extremely Orthodox Jews refrain from sex for a week after a woman's period. Don't ask me why. These are complex and archaic laws that I neither practice nor understand. Nevertheless, we are attempting a hybrid of this ritual. We have abstained for over a week. During this time, I've been playing a lot of racquetball and gorging on pints of chocolate ice cream at a single sitting. We will wait til several days after Ellen's period to what we feel (according to the thermometer readout) is the appropriate moment. Then try again. Thus, our quest moves from the scientific to the quasi-religious.

I can't stand it. Everywhere I go there are people. Lots of people. Turn on the TV, you'll see people. Turn the dial. More people. Pick up the newspaper or magazine. You'll see people. Go for a walk. People are everywhere. So how come it's so hard for us to add one more person to this collection? Obviously, not everyone has had this problem.

March 10, 1984

Have not been writing any diary entries lately because there's nothing new to write about. Nothing new. Nothing funny. Nothing traumatic. Nothing.

March 13, 1984

As I was in Chicago visiting Jeff, my best friend from high school, Ellen was in Columbus, Ohio, visiting Arlene, her best friend from college. Arlene, a mother of two, was delighted to learn that Ellen was trying to get pregnant and her advice was simple and to the point: throw away the thermometer and everything will work out fine. Three months is nothing. Don't worry about it.

Upon hearing this, I immediately felt better. More confident. My depression and sense of hopelessness vanished. Optimism took its place.

Odd how one can change one's outlook, one's frame of mind on whim. Why choose to believe Arlene's opinion over Dr. Lowell's scientific advice? Simple. I want to believe it. Perhaps the power of positive thinking coupled with an adequate sperm count are the keys to success in completing the mission we have undertaken.

March 24, 1984

Ellen's period is one day late. She took her temperature and it is higher than it should be, which means nothing to me, but which Ellen says is a good sign. We are filled with anxious anticipation.

Ellen also tried to pass off the extra few pounds she's gained lately (she's been eating a lot of cookies) as the beginning of pregnancy. I don't buy it.

March 25, 1984

Ellen is two days late with her period. Her temperature is very high, but she took her temperature later than usual so that may mean something, but I'm not sure what. The tension is beginning to mount.

March 26, 1984

Three days overdue. We're beginning to think that the semi-Orthodox Jewish method worked. However, Ellen's not sure she's pregnant. All this stuff about "Believe me, if I'm pregnant I'll know immediately" is out the window. Now I'm performing hourly breast measurements looking for growth in millimeters. We can't tell. One moment we think they're definitely a bit swollen. The next moment, we're not so sure. I'm her husband, I should be able to tell these things. Yet, they're her breasts. They've been with her for years, perhaps she would be a better judge than I.

If another day or two goes by and still no period, then regardless of breast fluctuation we'll be sure we're on our way.

March 30, 1984

For some reason we're awake at 6:00AM, and Ellen has a thermometer in her mouth.

"98.5," she says. "My temperature's remaining constant."

"Which means?"

"Which means my period is nowhere in sight. It's eight days late."

"You're smiling."

"Because I'm pregnant."

Freeze frame. The one that doesn't go away. Lily Cat is sucking on my t-shirt. Jester, slightly snoring, enjoys a doggie dream on his bed. My gray sweat pants, which need washing, hang over the back of the rocking chair.

"You sure?"

"I'm positive."

"You're so sure that I could call my mother?"

"I'm that sure. But let's not call anyone just yet."

And then there's a silence as it dawns on me.

"So we're pregnant?"

"We're pregnant."

"WE'RE PREGNANT!"

II
FREAKING OUT

April 1, 1984

For a woman, having a baby becomes a reality much sooner than it does for a man. For example, Ellen gives me up-to-the-minute body reports on the minor physiological changes that have begun to reshape her. Already she feels thicker around the waist and her breasts are larger and more tender than they were a week ago. There is a strange excitement within her. A little someone is developing. But we don't know its sex, its name, or what it will look like. She and child are partners in this process. But for me, the gestation period is something of an abstraction. As all sorts of changes are happening inside Ellen, I sit on the sidelines being proud, but somewhat removed from the action. I feel like the ambivalent football player whose team has just won the Super Bowl, but who didn't get into the game. I believe that until the kid pokes his head out and starts wailing and demanding to stay up late and watch TV, my fatherhood is mostly pleasant daydreams with no negative side-effects. I am further convinced that fatherhood won't become a reality for me until we bring the child home for the first time and put him in his crib.

In order to help bridge the gap between the concept of fatherhood and the reality of it, Ellen drew up a list of things we need to do or buy in the coming months to prepare for the day the kid comes home.

Ellen thinks we need: an L.A. ob/gyn (Dr. Lowell's practice is in N.Y.), baby clothes, maternity clothes, Lamaze classes, diapers, a washer/dryer, baby furniture, a car seat, toys, baby blankets, towels, washcloths, soap, powder, baby food, help (part- or full-time, so we can both continue working, so that we can pay for the above items) and a bigger house or apartment.

The information I'm gathering in these prenatal days adds up to my latest theory: Women think in images; men in numbers. Ellen envisions a three-bedroom house on the Westside, a maternity dress she can wear to dinner parties and designer baby jeans. She sees these things as clearly as if they were projected on a movie screen. All I see are long lines of numbers. Each preceded by a dollar sign. For now, those mounting dollar signs add up to my prenatal reality, the symbols that assure me that my wife's physical changes are not illusions.

April 3, 1984

So it's rest period between basketball games in Garry's backyard up in Toluca Lake, where about a dozen of us gather every Saturday morning to play games of 3-on-3 til we drop. We drop earlier in the day than we once did because now we're all in our 30's and 40's and our lungs and legs are not what they used to be.

Nevertheless, every Saturday morning we play the game, each trying to reincarnate the seventeen-year-old athlete who once resided in his frame.

So, we're catching our breath and sipping juice and Bo, who's in his early 40's and still possesses a deadly outside jumper, tells me that he retired a year and a half ago from his executive sales job in order to pursue a full-time acting career. His wife, whom he supported through graduate school, is now a psychologist with a full-time practice, and she is bringing home most of the money. So Bo says to me:

"We're living on half the money we used to, but it's okay. You really don't need that much money to live comfortably on . . . unless, of course, you have children. For a long time we talked about having a family, and I'm sure it would have been nice to have kids, but now I'm glad we didn't do it. With kids, you got to keep making the bread. Year in and year out. That's the thing about kids. They eat up your paycheck. And they don't go away. And finally when they're eighteen and they do go away, it's to college, and if you thought you busted your ass for a lot of years to feed 'em and

clothe 'em and send 'em to summer camp and to the ortho-
dontist, it's nothing compared to college. You know how
much it costs to send a kid through college these days?"

"No."

"For a good four-year college. Room, board, tuition.
Sixty-thousand bucks. And it's going up every year. How the
hell does a person save sixty grand and pay off the mortgage
and eat and pay the monthly bills as they roll in? How does a
person do that?"

"I have no idea," I said.

"I'm sure it would be a terrific experience to have kids, but
if I had to do it all over again, I still wouldn't have 'em. No
sir, from now on, I'm Number One. And my financial
worries are none. But, if I was strapped with kids, say one at
home, one at college . . . well, financially speaking, that's
murder. Hell, it's suicide. And what happens, if, God forbid
. . . ."

"Bo, what say we play one more quick game?"

Though I hadn't played long enough to be tired, I missed
all nine of my shots that game, then sped back to town.

Ellen greeted me at the door with a big hug. Her belly,
which I think of as being flat, pushed deep into mine and the
questions I had phrased and rephrased over and over during
my drive home no longer seemed worth asking.

April 5, 1984

Ellen called Arlene this morning and for the first time told someone else the news. Arlene, whom we consider an expert on the art of mothering and motherhood, told Ellen the following: do not go on a diet—do prepare to gain 25 pounds. Drink whole milk. Don't tell too many people (especially members of the immediate family) too soon, or they will constantly pester you. If there is a miscarriage, it will usually happen within the first ten weeks. If a miscarriage occurs, Ellen will have her period. (This bit of news was a great relief to me, though I pray it does not happen, for I was convinced that if Ellen had a miscarriage at eight weeks that I would walk into the bathroom one morning and see an eight-week-old fetus that slightly resembled me floating face up in the toilet, and I would have to fish it out and call someone from the county government to come take it away and dispose of it. And seeing this, I would flip out. I'm not being funny. I really imagined this. I mean, I'm not a doctor, how am I supposed to know about such things?)

That Ellen's breasts are getting larger and tender is a good sign, because it indicates that the hormones are going to work. And that it only took three months to get pregnant was a sign that we had strong egg and sperm. This, of course, was old news, for I've been confident of my sperm's strength for quite some time.

April 6, 1984

In a short and unsentimental ceremony, Ellen threw out her thermometer and temperature chart. One small step backward for scientific expertise. One large step forward for religious mumbo-jumbo.

April 7, 1984

Before going to sleep, Ellen looked around the room with an appraising eye.

"I figure if we're still living in these diminutive quarters when the baby's born, we'll put the bassinet in that corner."

"What's a bassinet?" I asked.

"It's like a cradle. It's what the baby sleeps in before he's big enough for a crib."

"I see. Are bassinets expensive?"

"What do you consider expensive?"

"BMW's, Georgio Armani suits and Haagen Dazs ice cream."

"All baby needs are expensive. They stick you good at these baby stores, because they know you're not going to do repeat business. I mean, how often is anyone in the market for a bassinet?"

"Surely some of our friends with children will sell us their baby stuff at a good price. Like David and Laurie."

"They've already given away most of their stuff."

"Without asking us?"

"No one in town knows we're expecting."

"Then we must immediately become friends with parents who recently had a child so that by the time we need this stuff, their kids will have outgrown it."

"But what if these people who just had a child plan on having another child?"

"Then I guess we have to make friends with a couple who've recently had a child and who plan for that child to be their last child. Or we'll make friends with a couple who've just had a child who will lease us the bassinet and crib and whatever else we need for as long as we need it."

"And where do you expect to find this good-hearted couple?"

"Bars. The classifieds. I don't know. We'll put the word out. Believe me, someone in L.A. wants to unload a bassinet."

"Great. I hope you don't mind spending your weekends driving all over L.A. bargaining with strangers whose children might be carrying God knows what infectious diseases . . . ."

"Okay, I'll ask my mother to buy us a bassinet. Now can we go to sleep?"

We kissed goodnight. Ellen lay on her back and closed her eyes. Lily, our orange cat, who sleeps under the covers and between us, moved across the bed to assume her nightly position. On the way there, Lily stopped and perched on Ellen's stomach.

"Hey, get off my baby!"

At midnight, I find myself yelling at a yawning cat. I think all this stuff is getting to me.

April 8, 1984

Ellen is freaking out. Suddenly, everything scares her.

I'm at the kitchen table eating an enchilada and reading the newspaper when I hear "Aaaaah!" and an "Oh no!" and a couple of "Oh my God's!". So I rush into the room, fork in hand, to kill the poisonous snake that I'm sure is about to strike Ellen dead, when I see she is reading an article about the pain of childbirth. And this particular article is about the unbearable pain a woman must experience while delivering, even if she requests pain-killing drugs. Because, according to his article, pain-killing drugs cannot be administered until a certain point in the delivery process. And that point occurs well after the internal baby gymnastics have convinced the mother that she would be feeling a lot better had she only waked up and run the Boston Marathon that morning, rather than waked up and gone into labor.

So I try to calm Ellen down by saying I understand. But, this is a big mistake, because what am I but a sex-starved heathen who has never once considered what goes on inside a woman's body. Or inside a woman's head, for that matter. I'm just like all the fathers who pass out cigars and call all the folks back home to spread the good news, while the missus, who has just dropped fifteen pounds in one hour, tries to figure out what the hell just happened to her.

Okay, I admit it. Men get off easy in the birthing process. Real easy. But, I refuse to personally take the blame for it.

"And besides," I tell her, "I'm going to be in the delivery

room holding your hand and wiping your brow and doing whatever it is they're going to teach me to do in those Lamaze classes. And when the pain is so incredible that I can't stand to see you suffer one more moment, and the doctor finally says, 'Do you want a pain-killer?', I'm going to roll up my sleeve and say: 'Please, Doc. I thought you'd never ask.'"

Though the pain of labor looms large in Ellen's mind, there is one aspect of pregnancy she fears even more.

"I'm going to get fat!" she said. "I'm going to gain twenty-five pounds."

"But you'll lose most of the weight when the baby is born."

"But til then I'll be fat!"

"You will not."

"I'll be fat and I'll be ugly and you won't want to look at me. And you'll want to go out with other women . . . and if you do, you can forget about ever seeing your child."

"How can you possibly think that I would be unfaithful to you?"

"Men do it all the time. Didn't you read Nora Ephron's book? Men get horny and feel neglected and feel sorry for themselves and go out with whores and upset their pregnant wives. And the emotional condition of the mother is crucial to having a healthy and happy baby. And if you go screwing around when I'm seven months' pregnant and I find out about it, and you know I'll know about it because I can read you like a book, rest assured I will become stressful and it will damage the baby's health. And if anything is wrong with my baby, it will be on your head, forever. But if you want to go out with other women because you impregnated me and now you think I'm grotesque, be my guest. I've always said, 'Do what you like. I'm not going to stop you.'"

On top of all this, Ellen has had nightmares about the baby's name. In her dream, she bore a girl and for some reason we named her Leon. And once it was on the birth certificate, we couldn't change it.

And since Ellen is older than the average pregnant woman, the chances of having a Downs syndrome child have dramatically increased.

And the child will like me better. And the child won't like her at all.

And what if this is a pseudo-pregnancy? What if she's not really pregnant, but because she wants to be pregnant, her body has been tricked into going through the physical changes of pregnancy? It happens.

Hey. I'm an 80's kind of guy. I'm attuned to my wife's emotional state. I know she needs to talk to me about her anxieties, that the worst thing is for her to keep her fears bottled up for the next eight months. But we'd better find some positive aspects of prenataldom soon, like settling on a perfect name or shopping for a bassinet or telling our parents and our friends the good news . . . . If not, Mr. Sensitive is going to freak out, too.

April 9, 1984

Are Slappy, Philo, Boaz and Ethelred appropriate names for the modern baby? Ellen and I have begun to play the name game and this is the kind of question that we are currently facing.

In the name search, we are assisted by a book we purchased that claims to list over 7,000 different names and their meanings. I found this astonishing, since every boy in my second-grade class was named Billy, David, or Joey, and I never suspected that Joey meant anything. And every girl in my class was a Mary, Debbie or Sherry. There were so many Debbies in my second-grade class that the teachers separated them by rows. They then became known as Debbie Row One, Debbie Row Two, etc., depending upon their distance from the blackboard.

I think it's important not to stick the kid with too common a name, and equally important not to give him too bizarre a name.

For instance, on my Little League baseball team there was an exceptional athlete whose last name was Doby. Fine name, except his father decided to name his only son Toby. Thus, our third baseman was Toby Doby. In batting practice, Toby was a hitting terror. Every third pitch sailed over the centerfield wall. But games were another story. As he dug his spikes into the batter's box and took his mighty stance, the P.A. announcer would proclaim, "Now batting for the Woolworth Red Sox, their third baseman, Toby Doby."

No matter how many times they had heard it before, everyone in the stands would crack up and Toby, humiliated by his own name, could not follow the flight of fastballs coming at him through his veil of tears.

Somewhere between the ordinary and the exotic, there awaits a name for our future child.

Our name search is half over. For if it's a girl, she'll be either Molly Bess or Lily Bess. These are name of relatives whom we loved and want to remember, and whose names we don't feel are too grounded in a previous generation. The kid will probably have more trouble with her last name than with her first. Ellen did not change her last name when we were married. I don't blame her. I didn't change my last name, either. So, in addition to having a first name and a middle name, our child may, if we decide, have both our last names. Thus, our daughter will be Molly Bess Sandler Danziger. Surely this will cause all sorts of problems, particularly when she goes to fill out her first credit card application and finds there aren't enough blanks for her name.

With all the warning signals in mind, we opened our book to the 3,500 boys' names. We only made it from A to I, because it is an exhausting process. And, of the 1,750 names we covered, the one we like best is Jesse. But this creates a problem, because our dog's name is Jester, and we often call her Jessie. I can see it now, the kid's four years old and I call out, "Hey, Jessie, time to eat."

I dump a Gainesburger into the dog dish and my only son races down the stairs and licks the plate clean before the dog has a chance. We like the name, but it could have negative side-effects.

So far, the other boys' names we like are Jonah, Alex and the ever-popular David. We have passed on such names as

Algy, Dempster, and Fagan. Perhaps we'll discover a name we love among the remaining 1,750 names. But I feel certain that no matter what name we decide upon, it will be one that sounds so magical to us that we will want to say it from the moment we wake until the last second before we close our eyes at night. It will be a name that symbolizes our shared love and affection for each other. And it will be a name that our child will want to change as soon as he learns to write.

April 10, 1984

The expectant father's thought for the day:

Is making love

to a pregnant woman

redundant?

April 11, 1984

One of the crucial decisions the would-be parents must make early in the pregnancy is choosing the right doctor.

We're set with Dr. Lowell on the East Coast, but chances are that the child will be born in L.A. So, we went OB shopping.

Back in March, Ellen had an interview with a Beverly Hills doctor whom she did not feel comfortable with, because he seemed rushed. This is the kid of guy she wants to avoid at all costs, the "time's money-money's time" physician who doesn't like to answer questions, because there are other patients in the waiting room poised to write him checks so he can spend August in Antibes.

Another type of doctor Ellen wants to avoid is Dr. Rigid. "Dr.-I've-Delivered-Two-Thousand-Babies,-And-This-Is-Your-First-Baby,-So-Who-Do-You-Think-Knows-More?"

She also wants to steer clear of Dr. Drugs. The physicians who are quick to inject chemicals when they're not really necessary.

Ellen's ideal OB would be a woman, favor natural childbirth, allow me into the delivery room for the entire time, not administer drugs unless absolutely necessary, allow the baby to be with Ellen immediately after the birth, and a doctor who would be with her, or whose nurse would be with her, for all of the labor.

Quite a few demands. Yet, the first place we checked out not only allows all of these provisions, they encourage them.

Jacqueline Snow, the nurse-practitioner whom we interviewed with at the Women's Medical Group of Santa Monica, and whose personality is the perfect combination of no-nonsense medical business gently balanced with a large dose of kindness and understanding, told us that if we wanted we could even have the event videotaped. We'll pass on that, but she did suggest that I give the baby a LeBoyer bath. I'm not exactly sure what this means, but Ellen thinks it's a great idea and I feel pretty sure I've gotten myself into the thick of the birthing process.

After our question-answer period with Jacqueline, we felt sure that we were in the hands of the best medical care we could hope for. Then Ellen was taken down the hall for a blood test. Since I'm trying to be a trouper, I went along to hold her hand and massage her forehead while Gwen, the nurse, drew blood. As I watched the needle slide beneath Ellen's skin, my stomach excused itself and left the room. And it was at that moment that I was struck by two simultaneous thoughts:

1) I am in no danger of becoming a junkie
2) If I start to lose my cookies while watching a simple blood test, what chance do I have of making it through the delivery?

Witnessing the blood test led me to thinking about men and their virility. Most men grow up teaching their sons to be macho. Macho is playing linebacker for the Pittsburgh Steelers, or riding a bucking bronco for eight seconds without falling off, or sacking a grizzly bear from twelve feet away or being chairman of the board and dominating thousands of lives. They think macho is showing no emotion and never, ever crying. Well, these men are real wrong.

Macho is holding your two-minute-old baby who's bloody and slippery and caked with birth gunk and giving him a LeBoyer bath without dropping him on his head or losing your lunch all over his tiny little baby feet.

This is what I call macho. And frankly, I'm not sure I'm up to it.

April 16, 1984

Ellen received positive confirmation today that the blood that Gwen withdrew from her arm last week indicated that Ellen was pregnant.

However, the same test also indicated that Ellen is not immune to rubella, German measles. Maternal rubella can cause birth defects, miscarriages and stillbirths.

So, there is more to worry about. Especially now, in Ellen's first trimester, when contracting rubella would, percentage-wise, prove most disastrous to the infant.

Since the main carriers of rubella are children under twelve, I must do my best to guard Ellen from small people with body rashes. This is not easy. What am I supposed to do? If I see a kid with a red, speckled face who is about to cough, do I jump in front of Ellen, block that cough, absorb the germs, quarantine myself and sweat out the disease until it passes?

In two days we'll be in New York City, and the thought of Ellen being packed in a subway car alongside people who are carrying, not only guns and knives, but also rubella germs is terrifying. We'll take taxis or walk. But only on those streets where there are no children.

Then, I think to myself, if Ellen hasn't caught rubella in the past, what are the odds of her contracting it now? Very slim. Though slim, another danger lurks.

April 17, 1984

"Then get an abortion!"

That line shot out of my mouth this morning at the breakfast table. Great way to start the day. Really lovely thing to say to one's pregnant wife, especially when I want to be doubly sure not to upset or provoke her during her first trimester, when a miscarriage, if it were going to happen, would most likely happen.

Ellen was expressing a legitimate fear.

"I'm going to be strapped full-time with the baby and you're going to go off and have a career and I won't be able to pursue my career at all."

So, what else could I have possibly said, but:

"Then get an abortion!"

Anything else would have been better. "It's raining again in Baltimore," or "This jelly is getting moldy." Anything but what I said.

It's still freak-out time. Ellen expresses a legitimate concern, and I push the panic button.

Why?

Because, perhaps, deep in the dark, typically male, "Father Knows Best" recesses of my mind, that's what I want. That would cause fewer problems. Fewer problems for me, that is. I would come home from work, pick up the kid, kiss him, play with him for fifteen minutes, hand him back to his mother and sit down to eat that homemade fettucine that the l'il woman cooked while the baby napped.

Except, that ain't how it's going to be. First off, I don't come home from work. I work at home. As does Ellen. We're two feet apart with our pencils and legal pads in hand.

So how are we going to continue working at home with a crying baby? I don't know. And who's going to take care of the baby when we're working? I don't know. And what are we going to be working on? I don't know. Hopefully a teleplay or screenplay that we can sell come June. But what happens if we don't sell anything? I don't know. And I don't really want to think about it.

And beyond our career as a writing team Ellen is a director. And what is going to happen to her career when the baby comes? That's where her fears lie. Is she going to have to give up her dream, part-time, forever, to be a mother? And how fair is that? Not very. But who wants to face such an issue? I sure as hell don't.

Being a one-career family in Hollywood, or anywhere else for that matter, is difficult. The boss for whom you've been working loyally for six years may suddenly not want to look at your face anymore. Or, the economy might go to hell in the next three months and jobs become scarce or non-existent.

And yet, we're trying to pull off a two-career/one-child household and, as I look around, I only know one other couple who have successfully pulled that off, but they were both very successful and well-to-do before they had their child. And we're not sitting so pretty in the dollar and cents column, but are just slightly ahead of the rent. And in this town, anyone can be chosen not to play in next season's game. It's all very scary. And so, when my wife expressed her legitimate fear that maybe we're taking on more than we can handle and maybe I don't want to think about things too realistically, I get a little edgy and say something I regret and that I'm going to be reminded I said for a long time to come.

And when you're wrong, like I was this morning, you're wrong. And then it's time to make amends, and just saying "I'm sorry" doesn't work beyond the sixth grade. So it's all got to come out. The fears and the craziness and the apologies and the confessions and the repentance. And maybe if I talk it out and I ask the right questions, I can be forgiven, but what I said will never be forgotten. Maybe I will wise up and express my fears and talk about them before they go jangly in my mind and I go pop and cause the person I love the most a lot of grief. Which, as I continue to find out, causes me a lot of grief, too.

April 18, 1984

Ellen has a job directing a play off-Broadway. So we flew into New York City this evening. For no additional charge, the airline flew our luggage to Boston. I was pleased to find out that my overnight bag would get a chance to see Beantown. It's one of my favorite cities.

Ellen's only possessions that made it to New York City with us were two green apples and one of our baby books, in which we read that at this stage of Ellen's pregnancy (six weeks), the fetus is 1/4" long and weighs less than an aspirin. And the fetus has already begun to develop its brain, nervous system, arms, legs, intestinal tract and heart, which is beating. All shorter and lighter than a Bufferin. It's too miraculous for words.

April 19, 1984

There is a rubella epidemic in New York City!

I don't believe it. I mean, I believe it, because Dr. Lowell told Ellen about it this morning at her appointment. It seems to have started in the South Bronx and travelled down to Wall Street. Within the past week, eight people on Wall Street have contracted German measles. And it's spreading at an alarming rate.

Dr. Lowell's advice to Ellen was to stay out of the Wall Street area and not to eat in restaurants. Coming to New York and steering clear of Wall Street is easy. But coming to New York and not eating in restaurants? This is cruel and unusual punishment. Also, the doctor told Ellen not to fly in her first trimester.

Twelve hours before her appointment, Ellen flies to New York only to be told not to fly and that the German measles are all over town. Oh yeah. And don't eat in any of the best restaurants in the world.

April 20, 1984

I called Dr. Pfeffer, our regular Los Angeles doctor. I don't think that's his official title. It's certainly not on his door:

I.S. PFEFFER
Regular Doctor

But we go to Dr. Pfeffer for checkups and routine problems. And before we got married, we went to him for our blood tests and I thought I recalled him saying something about rubella.

So I called him and he looked up our charts and said that both Ellen and I are definitely immune to rubella.

So we've got an internist saying Ellen is immune. And we've got an ob/gyn saying Ellen is not immune. Now what do we do? Get a blood test from a doctor whom we pick at random from the Yellow Pages and make it the best out of three? Frankly, Ellen is tired of having blood sucked out of her veins. And I'm tired of paying for it. But, no matter how many times we do a blood test, we're still not going to have a definitive answer.

If laboratories can make such mistakes on the simplest of blood tests, what are we supposed to think if the result of a future test brings us terrifying news? Or, what if they give us good news and it turns out to be wrong?

We've got to put our trust in someone. And we have. But when we get conflicting reports on what should be an objective analysis, we can't help but become alarmed and confused.

April 21, 1984

I feel like a mother. I don't say that perjoratively. But, of late, I've grown overly concerned about Ellen's eating habits. She's not eating enough, and she's not gaining weight. It's very important that she does both.

Ellen woke up late this morning. For breakfast, she ate a bagel with Jarlsberg cheese. After her midday nap, we walked up and down Broadway in the West 70's and 80's and stopped at Zabar's to smell the coffee beans and chocolate chip cookies and to buy some food for dinner. We settled on frozen ravioli and bottled tomato sauce and some eggs for a cheese omelette (foods not recently touched by New Yorkers who may be spreading rubella). We also picked up some potatoes and a cantaloupe and cottage cheese just to have around.

So, we come back to Peter and Kristin's (actor friends who are on the road) apartment and I cook. Since Ellen is pregnant and working, I'm cooking all the meals. Under normal circumstances I cook breakfast, which means pouring Grape Nuts into a bowl and slicing the banana. I also put the milk and vitamins on the table. And before Ellen got pregnant and gave up caffeine, I boiled the water and picked out an appropriate tea bag. All in all, I considered this a good day's work.

On some days, in addition to doing all of the above, I made lunch, which was almost as complicated a task as breakfast. On those days when I prepared both breakfast and lunch, I felt I deserved to be inducted into the Betty Crocker Hall of Fame.

Tonight, about an hour after we ate a substantial dinner that I prepared, Ellen asked me to bring her three leftover boiled potatoes along with the cottage cheese. I got as excited as a schoolboy preparing for his first car date. I forced myself to look cool as I brought the food, then retreated to the kitchen, where I spied on her as she swallowed bite after bite of starchy, white potatoes. When she dipped a potato half into the cottage cheese, I beamed with delight. Never have I been so happy.

In years past, I have grown ecstatic while eating white chocolate mousse, spinach gnocci or mu shu chicken. But never before this evening have I become physically aroused by watching someone else eat dinner.

I don't get it. I get my wife pregnant and I'm the one who becomes a Jewish mother.

April 22, 1984

Ellen sleeps. She also eats, reads the paper and works several hours a day. But mostly, these days and these nights, she sleeps.

Last night we went to sleep at 1:00 AM. We woke at 9:30. Any way you slice it, eight and a half hours is a good hunk of shut-eye. Ellen ate breakfast, read the paper, then decided she needed a nap. From 11:30 - 1:00 she sawed logs. At 1:15 she climbed out of bed and we took a walk down Columbus Avenue.

By 5:00 we were back from our walk and finishing our dinner. By 5:15, Ellen's yawning had so interrupted our conversation, that she would forget what she was saying from one moment to the next. From 5:30 til 9:00, she was back under the quilt.

At 9:00 she bounded out of bed and suggested we go to a 10:00 movie. Now I was getting tired. By 1:00, we were both asleep.

Ellen had slept fourteen out of the past twenty-four hours. She has not been bitten by the tsetse fly. But she is, by our calculations, around the 46th-48th day of pregnancy, which is when the embryo starts its transition into a fetus. Whatever is going on inside Ellen, it's wiping her out.

"He's totally taken over," Ellen said. "The baby's already controlling my life. I'm on his schedule. And all he wants to do is absorb my nutrients and sleep.

"He's got no respect."

"You don't understand what it's like. It's like I'm in a fog. Like I'm under water. When I wake up from a nap, instead of being alert and full of energy, I can't pick my head up off the pillow. It's just a horrible, horrible feeling."

Shortly after this passionate outburst, Ellen went back to sleep.

Though I'm alone most of the day, I don't feel lonely. I work on my play, read, take long walks, shop, cook, run errands. I feel needed. Depended upon. Responsible. For the health of Ellen and our child. It's a good feeling. Feeling grown up without necessarily feeling like an adult.

I peek into the bedroom. Nowadays, awake or asleep, Ellen appears to be relaxed, where once she almost always seemed tense. I, who edge toward the restless, the hyperactive, now feel calm, free of inner conflict. And, if I avoid watching the news, I can go all day without experiencing even a trace of anger.

It is odd. I don't know if we are urban hermits who must retreat to Manhattan to find solitude. Or if I am mislabeling all of this, and it is really the calm before the storm.

April 23, 1984

Today was the worst day of the pregnancy. The worst day of our marriage. The worst day of our eight-and-a-half years together.

Ellen conked out about 10:15. I stayed up to write, promising to be in bed by 11:00. Whenever I come to bed late, I wake her and it is hard for her to go back to sleep. At 12:45, Ellen rolled over, her hand reaching out to the space I normally occupy. The living room light, which I had forgotten to turn off, shined in her eyes, rudely interrupting her night's sleep. Awake, she bawled at me. I had intentionally left the light on, she theorized, suppressing my hostility over becoming her full-time cook, dishwasher and errand person.

And so, the psychodrama began. Ellen made charges. I made denials. Trying to quickly end it all, I threw off my clothes and climbed into bed, hoping the argument would pass. But Ellen was wound up and demanded to know why I had purposely left on the light. I stonewalled it. I thought the light was connected to a timer and would shut off automatically. Pleased with my excuse, I turned my back to her, told her to shut up and go back to sleep. A fist slammed into the back of my neck. I wasn't hurt, just mad. I reeled around and did what I have never done before. I grabbed her throat with my right hand, paralyzing her head, and slapped her across the face.

She screamed. I worried that the neighbors would hear. I

threw my head down on the pillow, trying to forget my actions.

We had fought before. Many times I had lifted her desk chair and with all my might flung it to the floor. She had taken my "works-in-progress" writing file, dragged it to the blazing fireplace and threatened to toss page after original page (not yet Xeroxed) into the flame. I had taken whole-wheat pancakes fresh off the griddle and thrown them at the walls and ceiling. She had clenched the L.A. Yellow Pages like a baseball bat and slugged a three-bagger against my chest. So we've fought before. We'll fight again. But always we respected our one rule: I am forbidden to hit Ellen. I'm 6'2", 180; she's 5'4", 110. It's like Ali fighting a bantam-weight. It's too one-sided. Too dangerous. I could do some serious damage. In a fit of anger I broke our rule. I've raged before, but this time I completely lost control.

When Ellen's sobbing subsided, I begged her to forgive me. She wouldn't. She couldn't. She didn't know me any-more. I didn't know me either. Not this me. Not the violent me.

I was the peacemaker. The guy on the sandlot who broke up the fights or kept them from starting. I was a good guy. Friends thanked me afterwards for stopping them from throwing punches. But I never fought. Not with my hands. I'd run. I'd laugh it off. But I didn't hit.

Now I had. I didn't know what to do. My apology didn't work. I hated myself. I dug my fingernails into my cheeks as if by ripping the skin off my face, I could erase my previous actions.

Ellen pulled my hands to my sides. When we both caught our breath, we talked.

I figured some things out. What I discovered was that I have a need to be perfect all the time and I will defend myself to the extreme against any criticism that suggests I'm not.

Admitting that I am human, like everyone else out on the street, perhaps as potentially violent as the thugs whose assaults and murders I read of in the morning papers, make me feel like dogmeat. But if I can understand that usually I'm good, not always perfect, not always right, but most of the time good, and admit to myself that there is also anger and jealousy and guilt and pettiness within me, maybe I can ease up on myself. So that the next time I am criticized or feel attacked, I will be able to react calmly and rationally, so as to keep myself from doing something really insane to my wife or my child.

April 24, 1984

Ellen started the day by leaving several thousand red blood cells with Dr. Lowell. Then she trudged over to Bloomingdale's and bought her first support bra. It's huge. She set it on the sofa and suddenly there was no place to sit.

Ellen's terrible night's sleep, compiled with the trauma of the blood test, added to a mile walk, the madness of Bloomingdale's basement, and her general fatigue, left her too weak to ride the escalator two floors up to the maternity department, where she could have justifiably dropped some big bills on bathrobes and nightgowns. But she was too pooped to spend money on herself. On clothes. From Bloomingdale's.

Though I see Ellen sleeping on the sofa or buried under the covers twelve to fourteen hours of the day, it was not until she shared this information with me that I finally understood the depths of her exhaustion.

April 29, 1984

Dale Wilson, a friend and a former high school basketball teammate, called me late tonight. It was one of those late-night calls I've always dreaded.

Dale, thirty-one, has cancer. The tumor pressing against his left eye is now spreading back toward his brain. He has lived with this affliction for two years. For a brief time it looked as if the cancer was under control. Now, all hope is gone. He has six months, maybe a year to live.

Dale is married, and he and Amy, his wife, have a daughter, Haley, twenty-one months. He wants to leave a videotape so that years from now his daughter can play it, and gain some sense of the father whom she never really knew.

Dale and I talked about how he might approach a videotaped farewell. How best to use the camera so that he will feel comfortable in front of it.

What a project to undertake. What do you say to the child you leave behind when you've only got a few hours of videotape? Do you address her as the two-year-old she is? Or the teenager or woman she's going to be?

I asked myself what I would say into that videotape if I were in a similar position. I would say, "I'm sorry. I wish I could be there with you." I would say, "I love you." It would help. But not all that much. Words cannot take the place of being there. Words and pictures are no substitute for a missing father.

Whatever I might say if I were in Dale's position could never express my feelings. Surely, I would feel cheated and rage at the Lord.

"Why me?" I would demand. "Why me when I am a decent and loving person who has much to live for and the scum on the streets go unpunished?" Or perhaps I would stop believing in God and in everything else.

At times I would no doubt want to end my life. Yet, I'm sure I would want to eke out every possible moment. But what for? Reading a paper, watching TV, shooting baskets would seem so futile. I would want intensity. Intensity of feeling, of love. I would be serious. Yet I would want to laugh. If I had the energy to laugh or to do anything at all. I know I would be angry and maybe even hateful of my closest friends who would be around to enjoy their lives, their children, long after I am gone.

But mostly I would hurt. Hurt for myself. For not seeing my child at all the wonderful stages of his life. I would hurt for his loneliness, for all the times he would need a father's love and counsel, and there would be none for him. I would hurt for my wife, who needs me and whose burdens would multiply if I were gone. I would hurt for my parents, whose final years would be filled with anguish for having to endure this most unnatural event.

I would try to figure it all out, justify it in some way, but know I never could. I would want to make it easy on those I love. I would want my friends to be especially kind to Ellen and to occasionally look after my child. Surely they would. At first. But, in time, normalcy would return. And with the regular flow of life, Ellen and my child would have to fend for themselves. That would be my final, sad realization. That I can enhance life in life, but not in death.

I am grieved by my friend's illness. By his suffering. I feel helpless. Small. Bewildered. I hug Ellen and we are grateful that at least for now, we are healthy. At least for now, it's not our turn to suffer.

I think of my friend, Dale, and in so doing, I think the unthinkable, which helps me to cherish life—a hug, a laugh, the morning light—a little bit more.

I wish I didn't have to learn of life from the pain that others endure.

May 4, 1984

The war comes home. It's my turn to take a blood test to determine whether or not I'm immune to rubella.

I am to meet Ellen at a West 84th Street address for a four o'clock introductory meeting with a theatrical producer. The clinic where I am to get my blood test is on East 85th. I leave Erin's Greenwich Village apartment (Peter and Kristin are back. Erin, Ellen's friend from college, is off to Europe) at 2:45, giving me what seems an excessive amount of time to make both appointments. The clinic is first.

At 2:47, as I stand on the corner of Greenwich and Seventh Avenue, it starts to rain. This is no drizzle either. It's Noah and the Ark time. I pop up the umbrella and wait. At 2:50, I hail a cab, but as I'm getting in, an East Side matron with a Tiffany's shopping bag cuts me off and she and my cab pull away. At 2:53, I flag another cab. The driver signals for me to meet him at the corner. The corner looks like Lake Erie. My shoes get soaked as I tiptoe into the back seat. I give him the East Side address and we're off. By 3:00, we're at 10th Street and First Avenue. We're making good time, sailing up First. At 3:12, we're up to 41st Street, but suddenly First Avenue around the U.N. is bumper to bumper as far as the eye can see. The cabbie lights up his third Camel of our jaunt and says, "This is crazy. Let me try going up Third Avenue." It sounds good to me. He swings left onto 41st Street, but then we stop dead. Forty-first is a parking lot. We creep along. The cabbie's getting crazier by the second. I'm cool. I still have plenty of time to get the blood test and make my four o'clock appointment.

"I can't make any money in this traffic," the cabbie says. "I'm going home."

"Not now!"

"After I drop you. Look at this. This is nuts. Fucking Mayor Koch. He's got people working on the Brooklyn Bridge, the George Washington Bridge." He goes on to name just about every bridge in New York City. "It's screwing up traffic something fierce. I can't make money driving in this. I'm going home."

By the time we've hit 41st and Third it's 3:24 and I'm thinking the shortcut was not such a great move, especially since the clinic is on East 85th and First.

"I've never seen traffic like this. Not at this hour. If it were 5, 6 o'clock I'd understand. But not at 3:30. I got to get out of here. I've been driving since 2 a.m."

"2 a.m.?"

No wonder the man's losing his grip. He's been locked behind the wheel for almost fourteen hours.

It's fidgety time. We're making about a block a minute, which stinks, and it's looking worse for making my date with the blood test. But I really want to get it over with so I can stop worrying about whether or not I'm immune to rubella. A friend whom I haven't seen in years works on Wall Street in the very building where the epidemic broke out and I'd like to visit her without fearing for my child's life. And I'd like to eat in a restaurant and avoid my own cooking at least once before I go home.

At 52nd Street, it's 3:42 and it's obvious I can't make my blood test. I reach into my pocket to get the producer's address.

"Where's 12 West 64th?"

"No way!" the cabbie screams. "No fucking way I'm driving you there. It's on the other side of Central Park. You can get out now and walk the meter, I don't care. But I'm not taking you to the West Side. Know how long it'll take me to get back to my cab company in Brooklyn from the West Side? Too fucking long, that's how long."

"Just drop me off at 85th, please."

The meter's up to $8.10 and the ticking of dimes . . . $8.10 . . . $8.20 . . . $8.30 . . . is making me jumpy. I want out of the cab, out of the rain, out of my 4 o'clock appointment and frankly, out of NYC.

At 3:52, at 65th and Third, with $10.80 on the meter, I pay the fare, plus a tip. I wish the cabbie a good weekend. I don't know why.

I'm a four-minute walk from the clinic, but if I go for my blood test, I'll miss my meeting. Ellen would have to take the meeting all alone with a producer of unknown ethical standards.

I stand second in line at the pay phone booth. Of course, it's raining. When it's my turn, I reach into my pocket and come out with a handful of subway tokens, no change. I cross the street and wait in line at a Safeway for a dollar's worth of change, then race back across the street to the phone.

I get the producer's number from Information. I dial and get the wrong number. My second quarter makes the connection. Ellen hasn't arrived at the producer's place. I tell him I'll be about ten minutes late.

My cabbie told me there was an 85th Street crosstown bus. I don't see one coming, so I look for a cab as I head west. Once I'm in a cab I should be at the producer's place in about seven minutes. No cabs. And the 85th Street crosstown bus appears to be a well-kept secret.

I pass Lexington, Park and Madison. On foot. At 86th and Fifth I spot the crosstown bus. I run to it. Just as I get there, the doors shut and it takes off. Still no cabs. I must walk across 88th Street through Central Park. It's about a mile hike. The sidewalk is one long, narrow strip of mud. As I walk, my brown dress shoes begin to look like melting fudgsicles. Sixty-sixth Street is flooded and as cars go past they spray me.

At 4:14, I'm across the park. The sun is finally out. And I walk the final two blocks, arriving at the producer's place at 4:19.

Meetings are like movies. You can tell within the first two minutes whether or not you're going to enjoy the show. This meeting has "Heaven's Gate" written all over it.

We share a few minutes of happy talk. The tenseness on Ellen's face says, "Let's get out of here as soon as possible." The producer says he has access to a small theatre in L.A. this summer and that the small theatre is going to be a hot ticket at Olympics time. He wants to put on a variety show. Ellen and I don't write variety material, but obviously this so-called producer has not done his research.

So, the man with the tan says, "Do you have any variety shows?"

Ellen and I look at each other. We're dumbfounded.

"Yeah, I just happened to have written one in the cab on the way up," I wanted to say. Instead I said, "No. Do you want one that is Olympic-oriented?"

"That would be okay," he says.

"Do you want music in this show?" Ellen asks.

"That would be okay," he says.

He sees we're not biting, since there's nothing to bite. He switches subjects. What he really wants is for someone to write a book for a Broadway musical or maybe a screenplay.

"And what will this book or screenplay be based on?" I ask.

The producer smiles and says, "I have the copyright to a lawsuit. I want to produce a Broadway musical or a major motion picture based on this lawsuit."

I'm praying that at this stage of development our future child cannot hear, because I don't want him to know what his parents sometimes go through to put food on the table.

We take the Xeroxed pages he hands us, say goodbye and wait til we're on the street and a block away before we crack up.

I rush to a phone booth. The clinic is open til 5. It's 4:52. It's remotely possible that I could grab a cab and if the traffic lights are with me, make it to the clinic on time. But if I strike out, we'd be an hour away from home by cab or subway, and instead of the afternoon being merely wasted, missing the clinic again would make the afternoon and part of the evening a disaster.

I opted to swallow my losses and we took the subway home, where, for the third night in five, I made another scrumptious dinner of frozen ravioli with bottled marinara sauce and salad.

Coming to New York City and not eating out is like going to New Orleans and not listening to jazz. Like going to Anaheim and not visiting Disneyland. Like going home and not visiting your mother. But that's our story for now.

When our kid is about six months old, I'm going to sit him down and tell him this story word for word. I'm going to play it for all the sympathy I can get. I will repeat the very same story once a year til he ships off to college. But I have a feeling my child will never really appreciate my tale of parental sacrifice until he is a parent himself.

May 5, 1984

Last night I had a nightmare.

I'm sitting at my kitchen table explaining to my sixteen-year-old son that the reason he's deaf is that one night during the NYC rubella epidemic I broke down and ordered some Chinese take-out.

I wake in a sweat, throw on some clothes, hop a subway and avert my gaze as a bored lab technician slips a needle deep into my vein.

In four or five days I'll know the results.

May 9, 1984

By far, the best aspect of being an expectant father is breaking the news to friends. I've done it in person and over the phone. In person is so much better.

I treat the moment of news-breaking as if it were part of a puzzle. It would be far too dull and anti-climactic to sit down with friends and blurt out, "Guess what? We're going to have a baby." So, I've established a set of rules for myself:

A. The announcement must be held for at least ten minutes after all assembled have said their hellos.

B. Everyone present has to have had his turn to speak about something that currently concerns him.

C. The announcement cannot be stated outright. Thus, to say, "We're having a baby," or "Ellen's pregnant" is against all rules. The announcement must spring directly from the conversation and the person or persons I am about to tell must un-wittingly deliver the lead-in line.

This is how the conversation went with our friends Lee and Connie when we stopped over to visit.

At the time, Ellen was carrying the rather dull lunch that I had packed for her in a brown paper bag. After the hellos, Lee and Connie, who were recently married, cracked out their wedding photos. We spent twenty minutes going through them, asking who was who and laughing.

Then Ellen says, "Excuse me. I'd like to go eat my lunch."

And Lee kiddingly says, "Are times so bad that you're brown-bagging it?"

Ellen and I look at each other, suppressing grins. Who's going to get to pop the line?

"No," Ellen says. "I have doctor's orders to stay out of restaurants."

"Are you okay?" Connie asks.

"I'm fine," Ellen says.

"Then what's wrong?" Lee asks.

"Well, there's a rubella epidemic in town," Ellen says.

"And you've never had it?" Lee asks.

"Right," Ellen says.

"What can happen if you get it?" Lee asks.

"Well, if you're pregnant, it can be real bad," I say.

Shock. Silence as Lee and Connie fill in the blank. And then we're smiling and hugging. Lee asks if we're kidding but knows we're not. And then he says he was wondering whether we were going to have kids since he knows how much we love them. And then we're asking them about their plans for a family and they're planning to start working on a little Lee or Connie soon and what is going on here is that we are sharing a transitional phase of our lives. Suddenly all us baby boomers have decided to make babies.

Our ebullient mood lasts for another half hour and then we have to hurry off. But a good, warm feeling remains. A reminder of what we're up to.

For now, sharing our secret with friends is the best part of the pregnancy. Only one aspect of our journey could top this feeling. When I make the phone calls to announce the birth of our child to our family and friends. I pray the event is a happy one.

May 10, 1984

I just got the word that I am immune to rubella.

This makes me feel great, because now I am free to eat out.

This makes me feel uneasy because one of these labs screwed up and I can't know for sure which one was wrong. Maybe the lab that just told me I'm immune is wrong.

This makes me feel guilty, for when I told Ellen that I was free to eat out, she said, "Go on. Eat in the best restaurants in the world without me. I'll stay home and eat a boiled potato."

This trip has been a bust.

A kid can really ruin a vacation.

May 12, 1984

It was a sunny Saturday afternoon so Ellen and I went to the Museum of Natural History to look at the fetuses.

There is an exhibit in the Biology of Man wing that explains reproduction in rather simple terms. Simple enough for me and the horde of twelve-year-olds clustered around to understand.

There were real fetuses from four weeks all the way through nine months on display. It wasn't gross. It was educational. It allowed me to visualize what sort of things were going on inside Ellen's body. It took some of the mystery out of the process. Judging from the exhibit, our fetus is now completely formed, but only as big as my thumb.

Reproduction is too complex for my unscientific mind. But a thumb I can understand.

May 13, 1984

Mother's Day.

I called my mom and my dad to crack the news. I was more nervous waiting for them to pick up the phone than at any other time of the pregnancy.

I told my mom that I had a Mother's Day gift for her, but she had to wait til December to see it. They were delighted.

I think the reason I was nervous is that this is the first time I openly admitted to them that I am not a virgin.

May 14, 1984

This is without a doubt the happiest period of my life.

May 16, 1984

I've begun to have conversations with my imaginary child. Sometimes my child is a three-year-old girl, other times an eight-year-old boy.

This evening as I walked on Broadway in the 70's carrying a bag of fresh produce for tonight's dinner, my imaginary eight-year-old son, Jesse, accompanied me.

Jesse is crazy for Italian food. Just like his old man. So when we pass a hole-in-the-wall pizza parlor called "A Brief Trip to Italy," Jesse nudges me and says, "Hey, Dad, you wanna take a brief trip to Italy for a little pizza?"

He's played this joke on me before, and I always laugh because he loves to make me laugh. So I put my hand around his waist and draw him against my body and give him a good squeeze.

"Not tonight, Jesse. Mom's waiting for us to get home with this." I point into the bag. "Which is dinner."

"Ugh," he says. "Another Nicoise salad. Why can't we eat junk food like everyone else?"

"Because your parents are weird semi-vegetarians. Life has dealt you some bad cards, my boy."

"It sure has," he says.

Later, as we're just about home, he says, "You know what I want to be when I grow up?"

"What do you want to be, Jesse?"

"I want to be just like you."

What a great little guy.

May 20, 1984

Back in L.A. Time to jump back into the Hollywood machine and make a living. Baby needs new shoes. Or will.

We told our friends Davey and Laurie the news. They went into shock. They actually froze for about ten seconds in wide-eyed stares like Saturday-morning cartoon characters. It was an especially pleasing announcement. Their two boys, Josh, seven, and Daniel, three, have been our surrogate children for years. These two feisty boys whom we love so much, who I once baby-sat for to get the feel of potential fatherhood, definitely influenced our decision to have a child.

Many times Ellen had voiced this fear: "What if our baby's not as cute as Josh or Daniel?" And I always say, "Don't worry, our child couldn't possibly be that cute. But we'll be so in love with our child we won't even notice. Or care. And regardless of the truth, we'll think our child is even cuter."

Davey and Laurie then volunteered their crib, stroller, car seat, changing table, all sorts of things that Daniel has recently outgrown.

The next day, Ellen went to see our friend, Cally, an acupressurist who recently gave birth. Ellen came back from her massage completely rested and carrying five baby books and a baby outfit that Cally's child has outgrown. Suddenly we need a chiffonier for baby's wardrobe.

I've never seen anything like this. This outpouring of affection between friends. I can imagine no other activity or announcement that instantly elicits hugs and kisses and gifts and all forms of emotional and even materialistic sharing. It's not like when something good happens to a friend and you're happy for him, but also jealous. When our friends hear our news, all their love rushes forth and engulfs us. It's all so wonderful and so pure and so overwhelming. Plus, it's saving us a lot of money.

May 21, 1984

I wouldn't say we're overanxious to have this child, but Ellen just asked me if I thought it was too early to pack her overnight bag for the hospital.

What are we going to do with ourselves in July?

May 22, 1984

We need a bigger place to live. Also, we'd like a place with a back yard. Or a front yard. Or a small strip of Astroturf so the kid can crawl around in the sunshine. Also, we desperately want to leave West Hollywood and head toward the Pacific, where you don't see the air before you breathe it.

This coming Sunday my weekly softball league begins. I love softball. Playing shortstop on a hot summer afternoon, throwing out a runner from the hole, is one of my three favorite things in life. But I've decided to hang up my cleats so that we can spend our Sundays house and apartment hunting.

I can't believe it. I've never done anything this mature.

May 23, 1984

We trooped off to the Women's Medical Group of Santa Monica this afternoon for Ellen's first one-hour comprehensive interview and examination. This included a discussion of Ellen's diet, exercise program, her prenatal problems (fatigue), our medical histories as well as our families' medical histories.

Basically, everything is still going fine. Ellen needs to take more vitamins and to increase her protein. Protein, we learn, is crucial for the development of the baby's brain. Thus, for the next six months I will be following Ellen around the house with six-ounce cans of tuna fish, wedges of Cheddar cheese and packs of sunflower seeds, nagging her to, "Eat. We want an intelligent child, don't we?"

Dr. Karen Blanchard, who conducted the interview, is a dream. She doesn't lay on any of that "I'm the great medical authority here" crap. She's more like a concerned friend who is also a scientist and an expert in her field. We're in great hands.

When Ellen told Dr. Blanchard that she wanted me to be in the delivery room, Dr. Blanchard said, "If he tries to leave, we'll break his arm."

Okay, so I'll be in the delivery room. I'm a man. I can take it.

When the interview is finished and it's time for Ellen to be examined, Dr. Blanchard asks if I'd like to come along to witness the procedure.

"Why not?" I think. "I'm a man. I can take it."

We go off to the examining room. Ellen changes into this two-piece paper examining uniform and lies supine on the table. She puts her feet in the stirrups and the doctor goes poking around with cold, steel instruments into the place that I thought was reserved for me. It begins to get a bit too medical for my taste and suddenly I say, "You know, I got a feeling that when my mother was pregnant, my father wasn't in the examining room."

They laugh as I move my chair over so that I'm shoulder-to-shoulder with Ellen instead of sitting behind the doctor, watching her perform these gynecological procedures.

As Ellen gets dressed, I realize that of the three people in the examining room, I am the only one who came close to fainting.

May 24, 1984

The memorial service for my friend, Dale, was held today in Houston. The doctor who gave him six months to live was five months short.

In Dale's memory, I wrote a $100 check to cancer research. The gesture made me feel stupid. A hundred bucks. It wouldn't pay for a week's worth of cotton swabs at Sloan-Kettering. Besides, what are they researching?

There's no medical cure for poisoned air, poisoned water, poisoned soil, poisoned food. Everything we need to survive has become carcinogenic. What chance do any of us have to avoid the Big C? What are the odds these days? One in four? One in three? Maybe I should pray for a heart attack during sex or a head-on collision when I'm 80.

I think of a way to protest, to make the world a tiny bit healthier place to live. I won't drive my car for a week. But as that thought forms, another thought replaces it. I have a 5 o'clock appointment. If I drive, it'll take fifteen minutes. If I bus it, it'll take over an hour, plus waiting time in the L.A. smog and sun. I'd arrive at my appointment looking like a pauper. No business would get done. I drive to my appointment.

I come home, look at Dale's picture in my high school yearbook. I remember how handsome he was before the cancer paralyzed the left side of his face. How his impression of Robert Preston in "The Music Man" always cracked me up. I remember his jump shot.

I cry. The way we all cry at funerals. For ourselves. Out of fear of being lowered into the ground. I imagine the faces of those who would attend my funeral if I had been buried today.

The one face I cannot envision is the face of my child. I am so anxious to hold that baby in my arms.

May 25, 1984

This is my latest theory, though it has flaws:

Brand new parents get a maximum of ten to twelve good years at the start. This is followed by twelve to twenty-five truly awful years filled with nothing but heartache provided by rebellious and pigheaded offspring. Then, if the parents are lucky, their children have children and the parents, now grandparents, get about two and a half more good years before it's all over.

May 26, 1984

Tay-Sachs disease is fatal. Always. It is an inherited genetic disorder that destroys the nervous system. For the first six months of life, a Tay-Sachs baby appears normal. When the disease hits, the infant loses his ability to grip, to crawl and to turn over. Later, the baby loses his sight, his ability to eat and to smile. All this suffering is topped by death, no later than age five.

Tay-Sachs is thought of as a Jewish disease, the way sickle-cell anemia is thought of as a black disease. The odds of a Jew of Eastern European ancestry being a Tay-Sachs carrier are one in thirty. In the general population it's one in two hundred. Since Ellen and I are both descendants of Eastern European Jews, we can add Tay-Sachs, like rubella and Down's syndrome, to the list of diseases that presently haunts us.

I went to the UCLA Medical Center this morning to get my Tay-Sachs blood test, which is where I was told all the above information. Since both parents must be carriers for Tay-Sachs to strike, I figured it was a long shot that our child would be afflicted. If my odds of being a carrier are one in thirty, I calculated that the odds of both of us being carriers are one in nine hundred. When both parents are carriers, the odds of producing a Tay-Sachs baby are one in four. By my figures, this makes the odds one in thirty-six hundred.

The doctor informed me that my numbers were all wrong. The real odds, he explained, were one in four. And it's a matter of first finding out if I'm a carrier. If I'm not a carrier, we don't have to worry about Tay-Sachs disease. But if the lab calls me next Friday and says my test is positive, then Ellen will have to be tested. If she, too, is found to be a carrier, there is a one-in-four possibility that the best course might be to terminate this cherished pregnancy.

III
THE BOOK OF
NUMBERS

May 28, 1984

It seems odd that the arrival of one approximately seven-pound, eighteen-inch baby means that soon we'll need 1,200 square feet plus a back yard in which to live. And, to acquire such a space in the City of Angels, we must be prepared to pay at least $175,000. Anything below that puts us in a section of town where it's dangerous to walk the dog at night.

For a couple who have as much chance of earning $7,000 this year as they do to make $70,000, the prospect of becoming a homeowner is terrifying. But, depositing our annual $7,800 rent into another man's checking account is nothing to brag about either.

The $175,000 house we walked through last night has no back yard, no front yard, no family room, no built-ins, no driveway, no entry hall, no guest house, no upstairs and is architecturally boring. But, for a mere $175,000, we are told, it's a steal and we should act fast and put in a bid.

We're mulling it over. It's more than we can handle, but the alternative seems to be moving to some distant L.A. suburb like Azusa, Placentia or La Canada.

I would feel a lot better if we had a job. Something that we haven't possessed in the past four months. Of course, if we wait til we get a job, this bargain house may be gone.

All this money for an eighteen-inch, seven-pounder. That's the size of a nice trout.

I think I'm going to start looking into mobile homes.

May 30, 1984

For the past 48 hours I've hardly thought about becoming a father. Nothing's really reminded me of it. I guess once the baby is born, that's an experience that will never happen again.

May 31, 1984

I received a letter in today's mail from the California Tay-Sachs Disease Prevention program:

Dear Mr. Danziger:

The results of your blood test indicate, within the accuracy of this medical test, that you are NOT a carrier of the Tay-Sachs gene.

ALL — RIGHT!

June 1, 1984

Finally got a loan from a bank. Not a credit union, but an honest-to-God California bank that charges high interest rates and makes you put up collateral and everything.

All this was pulled off in a quiet, end-run, against-business-as-usual-procedures move by our friend, Judith, who is a vice president of the aforementioned bank.

Being an honest, tax-paying citizen who makes an adequate living and pays his bills on time has never been good enough for a bank to loan me a dollar. Or for a company to trust me with my very own credit card. Even Sears turned me down. Though they did send me a complimentary air pressure gauge for my troubles.

So, hoping to become a model citizen and homeowner someday, I slide deeper and deeper into debt.

Boy, does it feel great.

June 3, 1984

Here in the second trimester, pregnancy has become uneventful, almost boring.

Ellen has regained her strength, and since she is not showing it's almost as if we've both forgotten that she is pregnant.

Twice a week she takes the Jane Fonda prenatal exercise class. I still chase her around the house, pleading with her to eat protein-enriched snacks.

Other than those occurrences and the fact that all of Ellen's pants are getting tight, things seem fairly normal.

June 5, 1984

My mother dreamed that Ellen gave birth to a healthy, blonde baby girl.

Call me superstitious, but if my mother dreamed it, I'm going to believe it. Even though I know my mother's dream is linked to her fantasy—having the daughter she wanted, but never had.

Still, choosing to believe there is some mystical truth in her vision keeps my mind focused on the positive, rather than obsessed on the infinite genetic foul-ups that could occur.

June 8, 1984

Income! Money for doctor bills and baby food. The four-and-a-half-month drought is over.

We got a job writing an episode for the TV series "KATE AND ALLIE." After our agent and Uncle Sam take their cuts, there'll be enough left over to live on for two, maybe three months. It'll get us through the hot days of summer without dipping into the savings.

The more money we can stash now, the less pressure I'll feel during those first few weeks of fatherhood, when I plan to retire temporarily and spend full time with my family.

June 10, 1984

With work comes fear.

It happens almost every time Ellen and I get a job. No matter how many scripts we've written in the past, no matter how many more we'll be hired to write in the future, when we first sit down to write, when page one rolls into the typewriter, panic grips me and I temporarily go insane. This leads to 24 hours of arguing, bitching, cursing and alibiing, which is occasionally mixed with a dose of chair-kicking and door-slamming, as I demonstrated last night.

This time, though, I went too far and put my foot through one of Ellen's two matching antique wicker chairs. She hated me for my tantrum. Accused me of not caring about her. And then she dropped the bomb.

"I don't want your baby."

She asked how I would feel if she destroyed this journal. That woke me up to the magnitude of her hurt, because that's what kicking her chair meant. They weren't just any old chairs. They were hers. She had picked them out especially for our study, the room where we spend most of our time. The chairs were her personal statement. I had no defense.

"When I'm upset, the baby's upset, too," she said. "Right now, your child is repulsed by you. Already the child is identifying with me and siding against his crazed father. Keep it up and you're going to have a juvenile delinquent on your hands."

I always believed that my father had made a number of child-rearing mistakes with me. But now, I'm committing mistakes he never even dreamed possible. With so many ways to damage an infant's psyche, I wonder how can I do right by my child?

The problem is, once I've admitted my mistakes and examined them and tried to correct my behavior, the damage is done. I may be all the wiser, but my child may be all the more angry and resentful of me.

Is there any hope that, despite my past and future sins, my child won't grow up to hate me?

June 11, 1984

Dr. Patricia Robertson, who introduced herself as Patty, felt on and around Ellen's stomach. Everything appeared normal, except for what Patty did next. She jellied Ellen's belly, then took something called a Dop-Tone, an instrument that looks like a transistor radio with an attaching microphone, and placed the microphone on Ellen's tummy.

WHISH! WHISH! WHISH!

It sounded like Larry Bird swishing three 20-foot jump shots. Or L.A. traffic. Or the surf.

What it was, was the amplified sound of our baby's heartbeat.

When she heard the sound, Ellen's face turned pink. She laughed and cried in the same moment. I rushed over and kissed her.

"You want to hear that again?" Patty asked.

"Yeah."

WHISH! WHISH! WHISH!

Up until that moment, there have been all sorts of unmistakable indications that Ellen is pregnant. No period since late February. Enlarged breasts and belly. Weight gain. Tired spells. And blood tests to verify her condition.

But it took the sound of our baby's heartbeat to make all of these things seem very, very real.

June 12, 1984

While lunching with our friends, Mimi and Larry, parents of a two-year-old Adonis named Cisco, our conversation turned to baby-naming. When we told them that Molly was the girl's name we had chosen, there was a strange silence.

Larry, who teaches junior high school and knows about kids and their names, told us that Molly is becoming "the" name for this generation of girls.

"It's not quite Jennifer," he said, "but it's advancing in popularity."

Lunch was no longer tasty. The last thing we wanted was a common name for our daughter. Molly was the name of my grandmother, of Ellen's aunt. The name has special significance to us. Why has it suddenly become in vogue?

Larry theorized that its popularity may have come from the movie "Annie" in which one of the more adorable orphans was named Molly. And though he was sorry to break the news, he knew of several newborn Mollys. In his apartment complex alone there were two.

Ellen and I came home and did some telephone research. We learned (after only a few calls) that some of the most boring people we know have given our very special name to their very average children. This irks me.

Even if we named our daughter Molly Bess, in time, out of laziness or out of our child's need to conform, the Bess would be dropped. Our precious daughter would sit in her second-grade class surrounded by a sea of Jasons, Jennifers and yes, Mollys. The thought depresses.

I don't think all these parents who stole our baby's name would consider renaming their kids. So, it's either live with the notion of giving our daughter a name that suddenly lacks creativity, or think of another name, or wait and see if it's a boy.

I feel the rumblings of competitive parenthood gurgling within me. The push to have a better, smarter, prettier, more-talented kid.

So this is how it all begins.

June 13, 1984

We looked in the Laurel Canyon area for homes. The part of the canyon we drove around is in the $180,000—$200,000 range. Most of the homes looked like Converse All-Star shoe boxes stacked on top of one another. The streets are narrow, winding and there is no place to park. The place reminds me of an area where the Manson family might have felt at home.

There's another part of Laurel Canyon, the glitzy show-biz section, where the numbers are much higher. There was no use in wasting the gas to drive up there.

House-hunting guarantees a devastating sense of failure. For no matter what you consider the ideal home, it is always going to be just out of your price range. Or in my case, several hundred thousand dollars out of my price range.

I'm hoping that our baby is born wealthy. I envision him coming down the chute clutching a Treasury note in each hand . . . .

Well, I'm allowed to dream, aren't I?

June 14, 1984

The seeds of competitive intra-family parenting were planted last night when Ellen asked, "What do you think the baby's first word will be, Ma-ma, or Da-da?"

I didn't know. Neither did she. But we both feared the worst. Baby would choose the wrong parent.

We kissed goodnight and pretended to go to sleep. But I knew that both our minds were racing. The kid will like one of us better than the other. It always happens that way.

Ask any parent which child is most loved, and ninety-nine times out of one hundred, you'll get, "Oh, we love them all the same."

Bull.

Parents usually have a favorite child. And children always have a favorite parent.

Ask a sibling, especially a teenager, which is his favorite parent and he won't lay any of that equality crap on you. A teenager'll tell you exactly where it's at.

"My mom's okay. I mean, like she's nothing special, but at least she tries. But the old man. Don't get me started on the old man. I could fill a book on him. But my mom, she's okay. Whatever she saw in my father, I'll never know. She must have been plenty drunk the night she said 'yes' to him."

So we're lying there, Ellen dreaming of hearing her "Ma-ma," me wanting to hear the magical "Da-da" or "Daddy."

Then I realized what I was putting myself through was stupid. For, no matter how hard we try to influence baby, he'll choose his own first word. And it'll probably be a word with no great significance, like "more" or "no" or "oats." But whatever he says it'll knock us out.

June 15, 1984

If I look at one more house (that I can't afford) I'll scream. We drove 82 miles this afternoon looking for an escape from West Hollywood. What's amazing is that of the dozens of areas of town we've studied, all but two are unacceptable due to a number of reasons.

The first, of course, is money. And what I still can't figure out is, who the hell can afford these homes?

To live in a two-bedroom, one-bath, Spanish-style home with a back yard not big enough to accommodate a decent game of catch in a neighborhood where people don't park their cars on their front lawns, is $200,000 and up.

That's $40,000 down and $2,000 a month til they cart you off to the old-age home. And that just gets you into the house. That doesn't include ripping out the lime green shag carpeting, turning on the electricity, hooking up the cable, plus hidden expenses that can surprise and take years off one's natural life.

Let's say I've been a good little boy and stashed $40,000 into a nearby money market (which I haven't). Then let's say Aunt Gertie dies and leaves me ten G's (which she didn't). Then let's say Ellen and I are both working full-time (which we aren't). Let's also say we're willing to invest one-fourth to one-third of all our earnings to pay off the mortgage. That means we'd have to be earning between $72,000 and $98,000 a year for the next thirty years to live in a decent neighborhood.

And I'm not talking posh neighborhood. I'm not talking upper middle-class or comfortably middle-class. I'm talking acceptable.

Either I'm crazy and totally out of touch with reality, or there's a real estate-banking conspiracy in the City of Angels that's robbing people blind.

I see the vicious circle, the dark side of the American dream at work.

1. Parents want to live in a decent neighborhood, so their kids don't grow up amidst dangerous people who have no respect for life, liberty or personal property.

2. In order to escape these undesirables, parents flee to the suburbs.

3. In order to pay the mortgage and maintain their new standard of living, parents must sacrifice a good deal of their freedom and work til exhausted.

4. Working this hard leaves parents with insufficient time to spend with their family.

5. The family, lacking the time for proper nurturing, becomes isolated individuals residing uncomfortably under the same roof.

6. The alienated children, sensing the unhealthy atmosphere of their suburban home and bored by the blandness of the community, seek out thrills among the very people their parents fear.

7. The children, bewitched by the mystery and vitality of these strange but intoxicating people, denounce materialism and move in among them.

8. The parent-child strain reaches an all-time low. Communication is impossible.

9. The children marry the very people their parents warned them about.

10. The children have children of their own.

11. The parents die.

12. The children and their family move into their parents' home, which has recently been paid off.

It doesn't make sense to mortgage my life for a house. On the other hand, it doesn't make sense to throw rent money out the window every month.

Two bad choices. I've got to choose one.

June 17, 1984

Father's Day.

No one called. No one sent flowers or candy. No one surprised me with a tie or a pair of socks.

However, my mother called and whispered a message onto my telephone answering machine:

"I assume you've been trying to call all day, but we've been out. Please call Dad and wish him a happy Father's Day. He doesn't know I'm making this call, so don't say anything."

I hope our child is more appreciative of his parents than my parents think I've been to them. But, why should he be?

June 18, 1984

I received this letter today from my mother:

Dear Dennis and Ellen:
We were very happy to hear the good news. Hope to God all goes well . . . . The only ones we've told the good news to are Aunt Marcia, Aunt Jenny and Aunt Lily. They were all so happy to hear the good news.
I didn't tell Shel and Sandy the good news, as I felt you should call them and tell them the good news. I know they will happy to hear the good news . . . .

I think I've finally done something that made my mother happy. Who would have ever guessed that it involved sex?

IV
AMNIOCENTESIS AND
OTHER SCARY WORDS

June 19, 1984

In eleven hours, Ellen gets a needle in the belly.

"Amniocentesis is a technique to collect fluid from around the fetus which can provide information about the fetus." So my printout from the Women's Group of Santa Monica reads.

In addition to finding out whether the child has Downs syndrome and its sex, the test also determines if the child has spina bifida, which is a defect in the bone covering the spinal cord nerves. A child born with spina bifida can have trouble walking, controlling its bladder and bowel functions. There are so many things that can go wrong, it's a wonder that anyone comes out all right.

Ellen has been relaxed all day and doesn't seem to fear tomorrow's procedure. Even I feel good about it. But since I'm not having the fluid sucked out of my stomach, it's easy for me to feel okay.

For some reason, we're not as worried about the outcome as we were, say, six weeks ago. I guess three weeks from now when we're waiting desperately for the results, it'll be nail-biting time again.

For now, we're just wanting to get through tomorrow.

June 20, 1984

"If labor is as easy as amnio, I have nothing more to fear," Ellen said as we drove home from the UCLA Medical Center.

Amnio came. Amnio went. Neither Ellen nor I watched the doctor insert the needle and, as usual, the shakiest person in the room was me. This, I realized, is because the expectant father is the only person in the room who doesn't have an active role.

The doctors and nurses all have their medical tasks to accomplish. Ellen, the recipient of all these procedures, has been transformed from person to patient and must carry out the doctor's orders. Breathe in, don't move, change clothes, sit up, hold your breath, etc. But I, the loyal and concerned father, have become a much appreciated, but unessential, handholder. I don't mean to disparage my role as support system, and I do think it's far better that I am there to provide comfort and to drive Ellen home than to forgo the event. But during the operation itself, I am filled with anxiety and fear and have no way of dealing at that moment with the emotions that the event brings. It would hardly be supportive of me, while amniotic fluid is being sucked from my wife's stomach, to lean over and whisper:

"Sweetheart, I hope you're not in pain. But I must tell you, all this is scaring the hell out of me."

Ironically, my anxiety did fulfill an unexpected need. Ellen became so focused on how she could help me get through amnio, that her fear as patient was displaced by her concern over my condition. Plus, she had one other advantage. She knew what was going on and how much discomfort the amnio was causing. I didn't.

Anyway, it was all done in less than an hour, including the sonogram, which was great fun. The sonogram, which takes pictures that look like fluid charcoal sketches, showed our baby moving around in Ellen's stomach.

The technician, who called our baby "the little gymnast" because he was bouncing all around his intrauterine playpen, pointed out the baby's head, arms and beating heart on the sonogram screen. Before we left, she gave us a still sonogram. An aerial gray-and-white photo of our baby's head. We have it taped to the refrigerator and labeled:

"Baby's first picture—minus six months old."

June 22, 1984

Remember sex? I don't.

I recall sex being something Ellen and I frequently engaged in before she became pregnant. But what sex is actually like? Tough question. I remember that it was usually good. But how it was good, what it felt like . . . very difficult to recall. Our doctors have guaranteed us that engaging in sex during pregnancy is perfectly all right. They gave us the green light to do as we wished. What they didn't tell us was that from conception onward, Ellen or the both of us would generally be too exhausted to get around to it.

Ellen's weariness is caused from working full days in addition to having a baby taking over her body. My lack of energy stems from putting in full days of work, plus taking over a number of Ellen's chores. Plus, there are new, baby-related areas like house hunting, doctor appointments and financial planning that eat up the time and sap the strength.

I appreciate our doctor's assurances that lovemaking can be an integral part of the pregnancy. But unless our doctors are willing to come over and cook dinner or help us find a bigger place to live, sex is one activity that's not going to get the time and attention it deserves.

June 25, 1984

When I put on my wedding suit tonight to attend a friend's wedding, I was shocked to find that the pants were tight in the waist. Real tight. Almost too tight to wear. This leads me to think that yet another aspect of pre-daddyhood has been completely overlooked. How come no one's ever written "An Exercise Guide for Expectant Fathers?"

We certainly are an unappreciated and ignored lot.

June 26, 1984

At present, I have one major fear: the results of the amnio. Yet Ellen's fears are not only more numerous than mine, they're far more creative. Tonight she felt a pain in her stomach and immediately asked:

"Do you think the baby is dead and decomposing in my stomach?"

"No. Do you?"

"I guess not."

"Then why do you ask such weird things that upset us both?"

"Because I think them. And if I ask them aloud and hear how ridiculous they sound, then I realize my fears are overblown. But it's good for me to say it and get it out of my system."

I wonder if being nuts during pregnancy can be scientifically measured. And if so, I wonder which parent would record the most psychic damage. I'm sure it would be a very close contest.

June 28, 1984

Scientists claim that the baby can hear in utero, and what he hears affects his behavior. For example, I've read that listening to Mozart or Vivaldi soothes a baby, while playing Beethoven or Little Richard makes a baby jumpy.

So Ellen, who thinks it's crucial that our child has a sense of humor, has just put Rodney Dangerfield's comedy album "Rappin' Rodney" on the stereo and she's standing in front of the speakers. Laughing.

It remains to be seen if listening to comedy albums in utero helps develop a child's sense of humor. But, if around age four, the kid looks up from his plate and says . . . .

"My trouble is, I get no respect."

. . . we'll know that the scientists were right.

June 30, 1984

Today we went to our friend's, Fred and Bonnie's, lawn sale and bought some nursing bottles, changing blankets, a colorful abacus for the baby to play with, and a denim Snugli, which is like a reverse backpack used to carry the baby against one's chest.

Today Ellen felt the baby kick several times.

Today Ellen ran into my arms crying, because she is so excited about having a baby.

Today we decided that renting a larger place for one year might be more financially feasible than buying a home and saying "so long" to our savings account.

Today I realized that when our infant spits up, or cries through the night, it will do no good for me to say,

"Would you please stop acting like a baby?"

July 1, 1984

Today's Air Pollution Report showed that in the metropolitan area, the P.S.I. (Pollutant Standard Index) measured two hundred, which means the air is unhealthful for sensitive people. I assume babies are included in that group.

It's not only depressing knowing that Ellen, the baby and I are all breathing poison (and that it gets worse every day), but it emphasizes the helplessness that I already feel.

As a parent, I can try to provide my child with love and security. I can teach him right from wrong and, by my acts, hope to set an example of how an ethical person lives. But the dangers of a poisoned Earth, of possible nuclear war, of violence in the streets, of freak accidents and of random encounters with insensitive and hateful people are beyond my jurisdiction.

Thinking about that which is beyond my control chips away at my ego. For in those moments I consider my helplessness, I am no one special. No one loved. I feel as if I'm just one more person who's using more than his share of nature's resources.

My skills seem so petty. My accomplishments don't make a dent. That I've come and will some day go seems to have affected but a handful. Maybe that's the reason I want a child. Visual proof that I was here. Evidence that in some way I made a contribution. That I counted. It seems a positive step in a negative world.

July 3, 1984

A brief, late-night exchange.

I catch Ellen studying her everexpanding body in the mirror.

"What are you thinking?"

"I know this is going to sound crazy," she says, "but I never really thought I'd get big like this. And I'm not sure I'll ever get used to it."

"What did you think would happen when you got pregnant?"

"I don't know. I guess I was hoping that for the first eight months I'd look like Lauren Bacall. And in the ninth month, I'd get fat and have a baby. Of course I know that when women get pregnant, they get big, but somehow I didn't think it would happen to me."

"It's all you. It's just a bigger, better you."

"You sound like you're describing a laundry detergent."

"I think you look great."

"Maybe so," Ellen said, checking the mirror, "but it sure doesn't look like me anymore."

And later, just as the lights went out:

"You're not going to run around on me now that I'm all fat and out of shape?"

"No. Never."

And we kissed goodnight.

July 4, 1984

Last night, for the first time, I saw my child in a dream. But my child was no longer a child. She was twenty-one and the leader of a singing group that was playing to a standing-room-only crowd in a basketball arena.

Though the group she was a part of played folk music, my daughter never sang, she just kept tuning up and would occasionally step up to the microphone, say something funny, crack everyone up and go back to tuning up.

Every time she stepped up to the microphone, I saw her face, yet didn't think she resembled either Ellen or me. But on the third look, I realized she had my broad, awning-like forehead and Ellen's high cheekbones and thin face. Her hair was brown like mine, and was combed up and back and fell in waves to her shoulders.

She was lovely, but not a knockout, which I thought was good, because being gorgeous is often a disadvantage. I never heard her sing, but she made me laugh and made me proud.

The really odd thing was that when I began to tell Ellen my dream, she said that she also saw our child for the first time in her dream last night, though she remembered very little except that it was still an infant and it was a girl.

So Ellen, my mother and I have all dreamed that the baby is a girl. Judith, our banker, has a theory that in odd-numbered years, all her pregnant friends give birth to boys and in even-numbered years, girls take over.

We're "four and oh." I guess it's going to be a girl.

July 5, 1984

Just before noon, the phone rang. It was Vivian from the Women's Medical Group.

"Is Ellen there?"

"No. Can I take a message?" I asked.

"I have some test results."

"From the amnio?"

"Yes."

"This is her husband. Is it good news or bad news?"

"It's good news."

I forget the exact words that followed, but the results of the amnio showed that the baby did not suffer from any disease that the amnio could detect.

Our child, to this point, as far as medical science can predict, is healthy.

"Do you want to know the sex?" Vivian asked.

"We have an afternoon appointment. Please tell us then."

I always imagined we'd both be home when the results came in and we could celebrate or mourn together. But since Ellen had gone to her exercise class, I was left along to jump up and down over and over, hug and kiss my dog and say,

"Jester, the baby's healthy! The baby's healthy!"

The dog took it in stride. I cried.

Crying and worrying about money must be the chief activities of all expectant fathers.

When Ellen and I arrived at the doctor's office, Vivian asked us how we wanted to get the news.

"In private," was our answer.

She wrote it on a piece of paper and folded it in half. We took it into Dr. Blanchard's office, sat on the sofa, held hands and one of us, I forget who, unfolded the paper, which read:

CONGRATULATIONS! IT'S A BOY!

We hugged. We kissed. And then, of course, we cried.

July 6, 1984

We made a big mistake.

We should not have learned our baby's sex. Suddenly, the drama of the pregnancy is over. The miraculous has become the mundane. The surprise nature had in store for us has been usurped. The structure of the pregnancy, the crisis of labor, the climax of birth, the denouement of learning the baby's sex, has been shattered. We have taken the ultimate mystery out of the process and, in so doing, robbed ourselves of months of suspense and speculation, as well as depriving ourselves of time to revel in our good fortune that our baby is healthy.

Just the other day a friend asked if we'd insist on being told the baby's sex.

"Of course," I said. "I want to start calling our baby by name, rather than 'it'."

He couldn't understand why anyone would want to know the sex prior to birth. I couldn't understand how anyone could stand not knowing. For me, the curiosity would be too overwhelming.

And though there are some positive aspects of knowing the sex, I now wish we had refrained from asking.

V
HALF WAY HOME

July 12, 1984

Today is the one-hundred-fortieth day, the unofficial halfway mark of the pregnancy. Many of Ellen's friends who are mothers have told her to treasure her months of pregnancy, for they will be over before she knows it. Maybe so.

But to me, the first twenty weeks, which have been filled with panic as well as joy, seem to have taken forever.

July 16, 1984

Every day now, Ellen feels the baby kick.

This morning at breakfast she flinched to attention and said, "The baby's really busy today. It feels like he's moving furniture around in there."

I put my hand on her stomach and held that position for ten minutes, hoping to feel a kick. But my son refused to oblige me. Of course, the moment I took my hand away, Ellen laughed and said, "He's doing it again. It feels like he's playing handball inside me." I put my hand back, but again it was too late.

Seems the boy will do anything to delight his mother. Of course, he and his mom already have a strong thing going. But if I want something from my son—well, I guess I'm going to have to wait til he's here and earn it.

July 18, 1984

We've got the crib. It needs a paint job. It needs a mattress and bumper pads and sheets. But we've got it.

The crib is unassembled and leaning against the wall under the staircase, where I catch a glimpse of it every time I leave my study and go to the kitchen for a snack. On those frequent breaks, I stop and stare at the headboards, the sideboards, the metal frame. Four and a half, five months from now, my son, this stranger who I'm dying to meet, is going to be sleeping in that crib. Or crying or laughing or throwing his toys out onto the floor for me to pick up.

I guess this is really going to happen.

July 19, 1984

What expectant parents really think:

Ellen:	**Dennis:**
	Honeymoon Night:
I want to get pregnant.	I want to have sex and if you get pregnant, that's okay, too.
	Postconception
I pray it's not twins.	If it's a girl, what do I talk to her about for the next 18 years?
	On Learning the Baby's Sex
This little guy better like shopping for clothes.	What do I do with him if he doesn't like baseball?

FUTURE PLANS:

Undergraduate School

Harvard, Brown or near-equivalent	Stanford (if he gets a scholarship). Otherwise community college.

Graduate School

Harvard Law	Forgoes grad school—is drafted third round by Boston Red Sox.

Honors

LL.B. Harvard Law	AL Rookie of the Year-2005

Real Life

Gives up law, becomes an architect/interior designer (redoes mom's home—for cost of materials only)	Gives up baseball after making millions to become political correspondent for CBS News.

Dream for Parents' Old Age

Cooks gourmet meal every Sunday at his parents' house.	Still talks to me.

Would Settle For

A lovely daughter-in-law who cooks gourmet meals every Sunday at her in-laws' house and two gorgeous grandchildren.	A CPA who stays out of jail.

July 23, 1984

Ellen made this week's issue of Newsweek magazine!

Accompanying an article entitled "Now, the Pregnancy Workout" is a photo in which Ellen, wearing a plum-colored leotard, stretches alongside several other full-bellied women.

One of these years when our boy is saying all sorts of things we'd rather not hear, like "You don't love me, you never loved me," I'll just open the family album to the photo and say, "You know how mom hates to exercise? Well, look at her. Busting her chops in this hot, smelly gym so you wouldn't suffer too much during birth. Now how can you say we don't love you?"

To which he'll reply, "Okay, so mom loves me. But you don't."

I've got to get my picture in a national magazine before he's born.

July 24, 1984

The second trimester is incredibly boring. To pass the time, I daydream.

Today, I married off my son, twenty-six, to a D.C. lawyer, twenty-eight. I approved the marriage. She was smart and had a good job. I was almost sixty and couldn't believe my time was almost over.

Today I lay on the sofa with my sleeping infant resting on my chest, not believing something so wonderful as this little boy could happen to me.

Today, on a rural New Hampshire road, I pulled the car over, got out, flipped the keys to my fourteen-year-old son and told him to get in the driver's seat and buckle up. It was time he learned to drive.

Today I watched him graduate high school, get his first Little League base hit. I heard him yell at me, call me "stupid and old-fashioned." I saw him hospitalized with six broken ribs as a result of a car wreck, go to Europe and not call or write for months at a time. I witnessed him changing his name so it wasn't mine and putting his arms around me and saying, "You know, for a guy your age, you're not half bad."

I just wish he'd hurry up and get here so some of these things could start happening.

July 27, 1984

Since the beginning of the pregnancy, I, like most expectant fathers, have gained weight. I fluctuate between gaining three or four pounds, then I diet and lose them, but quickly the pounds return.

I have several possible explanations for this: 1) Sympathetic weight gain, 2) Lack of regular exercise, or 3) A less-active sex life causing anxiety and leading to a terminal case of "the munchies."

Before going to bed last night, I checked in the mirror and I seemed to have returned to my prepregnancy physique. But during the night I had a dream. For the first time ever I had a beer gut. My thirty-four-inch waist had popped out like a six-month-pregnant woman's stomach. And then, as I looked in the mirror again, it dawned on me—I was pregnant.

Psychiatrists, to your marks!

July 28, 1984

Ever since Ellen's stomach "popped out" a few weeks ago, she has been feeling weird and unattractive.

She says she feels fat and schlumpy and, no matter what she puts on, she complains that it makes her look like a clown or a woman wrestler. But after an expensive, three-hour shopping binge this afternoon, which added three blouses, one skirt, a pair of shoes and lots of other stuff she can wear regardless of her condition, she now feels "pregnant chic" and her blues have washed away.

Seems spending money on maternity clothes that don't look like maternity clothes is a sure-fire anxiety buster. I wish one of us had thought of it sooner.

August 4, 1984

It is our last nomadic, come-and-go-as-you-please vacation (with a side of work). A play of mine is being given a staged reading at the Summer Solstice Theatre Conference in East Hampton. Ellen is directing.

Within the space of ninety-six hours, we flew from L.A. to NYC, found ourselves locked out of our friend Jane's apartment, where we had intended to stay, were adopted by and spent the night with Chaim and Sophie, our friend's next-door neighbors whom we had never met, fled the city due to incredible heat and humidity, bused out to Long Island, where our days are intense with work and our nights are filled with the catch-of-the-day, plum pie and aimless walks on the Amagansett Beach.

We have complete freedom. Our major responsibilities are to feed our faces and to get a good night's sleep. It's the best trip we've ever been on. But I do not know for sure whether our good times are being intensified because we know that the next time we leave home, we'll be toting a baby and his accessories and our time will not be our own. Or perhaps our present euphoria is due to residing in a place that feels like Paradise combined with the eager anticipation of becoming parents.

Whichever, I am savoring the moments. And for the moment, being childless, yet almost a father, is a fine place to be.

August 11, 1984

The sixth month, the end of the second trimester, is so uneventful that there is absolutely nothing to report.

August 13, 1984

I am standing in line at the half-price theatre tickets line on an esplanade in the middle of Times Square. Ellen is out having lunch with a friend, and the question that continually arises is, "What would we be doing right now if the baby were here?"

And the constant refrain is: "We wouldn't be doing what we're currently doing." At least, not both of us. And though I know in my mind that the baby, as everyone says, "is going to change everything," I cannot grasp the full meaning of that, and surely won't comprehend it until the little guy is in hand.

August 15, 1984

Ellen is beginning to experience a dose of backache, particularly when she sleeps.

I give her nightly massages, which temporarily solve the problem, but during the night, usually around 4 a.m., she gets out of bed and relocates to the sofa. Her middle-of-the-night move does not disturb me, but I do wish I could be of more help.

But as long as Ellen is carrying around what appears to be a 12-pound bowling ball, Nature will continue to slow her down, make her ache. And what I have found is that I am no match for Nature.

August 17, 1984

I find myself two or three steps behind Ellen as she moves instinctively around Bloomingdale's infant department, inspecting its wares.

Ellen, who has done her baby research, understands the function of almost every item, yet I am perplexed by almost everything I see. What are Gum Soothers and why must they be refrigerated? Are Ducky Diaper Pins really necessary? In addition to the crib, do we need a bassinet? A playpen? A supersonic 24-hour battery-operated swing? A Kanga-Rocker-Roo?

A saleswoman describes the strollers, which start at $180 and soar to over $300. She tells us that the most expensive stroller was designed by a Japanese man who also designed airplane seats. I tell her that our baby is going to be pushed, not flown, most places and does she have anything for about $150? She raises an eyebrow and excuses herself to answer a phone.

I inspect the goods. Bottle warmers. Water toys. Rattles. Clothes. I hear myself saying, "When I was a kid, t-shirts cost ninety-eight cents, not $12.95."

A guy about my age, who is every bit as dazed as I am, looks over at me. His pregnant wife holds up a pair of corduroy baby overalls. She is pleased with the overalls and will definitely buy several pairs. Her husband, grim-faced and glassy-eyed, nods at me. I nod back. We are silent comrades, lost in a game we entered without first learning all the rules.

August 24, 1984

Back in L. A., looking for suitable housing. To rent, not to buy.

We drive 75 miles a day travelling from one duplex to another, looking for the perfect breakfast nook. A thousand dollars a month rents a two-bedroom, one-bath half-a-home in not too safe a neighborhood. God, it's depressing.

To top off the day, the woman we desperately wanted and had planned on hiring as our baby-care person refused us, saying she can make more money continuing to clean houses.

All of my energy and Ellen's energy is channelled into getting ready for baby. We cannot get to our other work. The kind that sometimes makes money. It's exhausting, defeating, frightening.

Before Ellen dragged her body off to bed, I gave her a hug, then whispered into her belly, "It's worth it. I know it's all worth it."

August 28, 1984

We found a great place to live! It's not in Bel Air, or in the hills of Santa Monica, or on the beaches of Malibu. Actually it's only fifteen blocks from where I sit. But it's fifteen long blocks from the male prostitutes who hang out on Santa Monica Boulevard, fifteen blocks from the punkers, the drug peddlers and the runaways. Fifteen blocks from the amateur rock musicians who've spent thousands on equipment, but never a penny on lessons. Away from the midnight chanters, the all-night screamers and the nuts who vacuum at 5 a.m.

My son's first home, which he won't remember, is located in a dull, residential, middle-class neighborhood, filled with retired couples who turn off their TVs early, ambitious junior executives who stay up late working and married couples like us who'll be too tired to do anything more strenuous than bathe after 8 p.m. It will be marvelously boring. I can't wait.

Of course, our rent's rocketing, a $350-a-month increase, and I can't quite believe the size of the numbers I'll have to write on each month's check. But it's worth it.

For the first time since I've moved to L.A., I won't have to park on the street where any hit-and-run driver could smash into my car, which happened just yesterday morning to the tune of $512. Of which my insurance company covers those last twelve dollars.

It's the little things like babies and hit-and-run drivers that motivate one to flee a neighborhood. And flee we will on October 1, into our new rental home where we'll decorate the back bedroom with colorful posters and mobiles and other stuff we haven't yet bought.

It's nothing splashy, this new place. But it's light and airy and calming. We'll feel good living there.

And I'll feel good, because I swore I wouldn't bring our child back to this tiny house on this mean city street. And having lived up to my expectations, this father will bring his firstborn home feeling not like a failure, but like a king.

VI
JUST WHOSE BABY IS IT?

September 2, 1984

Just whose baby is it?

I was under the assumption that the child we are expecting is ours. Ellen's and mine. But depending upon whom I speak with, all that changes. Suddenly, there are other people laying claim to our son. And perhaps in time still more people, people who at the moment I don't even know, will insist they own stock in our boy.

This thought came to mind only minutes ago during a conversation with an unnamed party who is carefully monitoring Ellen's pregnancy. Oh, why hide it? It's my mother.

And so, my mother says, "The names you have chosen are perfectly all right with me. I wouldn't want you to change them."

Which means she doesn't love the names and might like us to change them, but she'll let it go without a fight.

And so I learn, months before I am officially a father, that others think they have rights regarding my child. And perhaps they do.

Not only do parents and grandparents think they possess the child, but I understand that nannies and baby-care people often fall in love with the child they are raising. And when their services are no longer needed and it comes time to say goodbye, they suffer as if they were abandoning their own flesh and blood.

And on it goes. Just whose baby is it?

And if one believes that there is a divine Creator, as I do, then one realizes that although two fourteen-year-olds might be perfectly capable of reproduction, that something far more intelligent and powerful and awesome dreamed up creation.

And, if this is so, then perhaps the child who we are bringing into the world is ours to teach, and to love, and to care for, but ultimately this child is God's creation, and we are blessed with this child's presence for a day, a week or hopefully and selfishly, all the days of our lives.

For how can I really say that he is my child? I am not so arrogant to think that I am such a creative force. Six months ago, I was needed for a few moments to send some semen upstream, and then my job was done. Some creator.

Ellen carries the developing fetus. But, inside her, he grows. The creation creating himself. How astonishing that this creature who has never existed, who started as a single cell, somehow knows how to evolve into the person he is to become.

Ellen supplies him with tuna fish and peanut butter. But she has no say over how big he is becoming, or when he's coming out. Like it or not, the child eats, he kicks, he keeps her up nights. He has a life of his own, which only he, not his folks or grandfolks, possesses.

Soon we will diaper him, talk to him, feed him and love him. We have a responsibility towards him. We participated in his being. But there will come a day when he is more in control of his life than we are. When he is his own person. When he will say which of us has a claim to him. If any of us has a claim to him at all.

September 3, 1984

Why is it when people who are parents say, "When your baby comes, everything is going to change," they have a demonic gleam in their eye?

September 7, 1984

Today is the first day of the third trimester. Instead of counting how long the pregnancy has lasted, we are now counting backwards. There are only eighty-five days to go.

As the delivery date nears, the pressure mounts to get ready for baby. Move and set up the nursery, install the car seat, take a tour of the hospital, go to childbirth classes, etc. But the reality of being a father, of actually holding my child in my arms, of waking at 2AM to feed him, of changing his diapers, remains a distant dream.

September 10, 1984

According to my research, if our baby were born alive, in this the seventh month, he would have better than a fifty-percent chance of surviving. It is a fact often on my mind.

September 11, 1984

I am drunk. And angry.

We lost the house. The people won't rent to us, because we have a dog. At first, they wouldn't even consider us, because we were expecting a child. But then, having interviewed what was obviously a long line of unsavory Americans, they had a change of heart and called us back. Suddenly, it was okay to bring life into the world. Or, at least, into their house for one year.

After they interrogated our previous and present landlords, checked our references and studied our bank balance, they agreed to have us. They liked us. They trusted us. Then, we mentioned the dog. You'd have thought I'd pulled out a gun.

"What is wrong with this couple?" they must have thought. "A child and a dog? What are they, an orphanage, they have to be surrounded by so many living things?"

We offered to put down a $2,000 deposit. They wouldn't hear of it. There are no carpets, no drapes in this house. There's nothing for our dog to destroy. "Let me introduce you to our dog," I pleaded. "See how tame she is."

Nope. A child and a dog. These people are obviously off the wall. We'll rent to people who'd never consider adopting a pet or bringing a child into the world. We'll rent to people whose only responsibility in life is to themselves. We'll rent to people who come home and sit in the very same chair night after night and drink a beer, watch TV and then quietly go to bed. Anybody but a couple who have a baby and a dog. Good God! (And I didn't even tell them about the cats.)

May their home lie on the San Andreas Fault and be sucked to China when the Big Quake hits.

Better yet, may they go through life without knowing what it's like to love a dog, or a cat, or a child.

September 12, 1984

I flunked the Glucola test. Which is odd, because I didn't even take the Glucola test. Ellen did.

All pregnant women must be checked for diabetes and, in order to do so, Ellen had to drink a bottle of Glucola, ten ounces of what looks like Nehi orange soda. Except that it's much sweeter than soda, and you won't find it in the cooler at your neighborhood 7-Eleven.

Knowing that from 8:00 to 8:05 this morning she would have to drink all 10 ounces, Ellen prepared by having Glucola nightmares and losing hours of sleep. She woke up exhausted and scared.

By 8:15, she was still hiding in bed, pretending to sleep. So I, the drill sergeant, commanded her to march downstairs and swallow her medicine like a soldier.

By 8:25, Ellen sat at the kitchen table, facing the opened Glucola bottle and a glass filled with ice. By 8:26 she had taken one petite sip and made a face. At 8:28, I took a taste and proclaimed, "It's just like orange pop. What's the problem?"

By 8:30 I had told her that I was ashamed of her behavior, and if she couldn't knock down a bottle of pop, how the hell was she going to handle labor? Then I took the dog for a fifteen-minute walk because, like General Patton, I can't stand being around people who are feigning weakness of the stomach or heart.

When I returned and saw how the whole experience had frightened and nauseated her, it hit me. Just because I'm a man who could chug-a-lug a whole case of Glucola for the sheer hell of it, doesn't mean I can control Ellen when she has to take a dozen sips of it. And, finding myself unable to control her, I walked. Instead of finding the strength to hang in and support her and help her through what to me was a simple task, but to her was a painful and upsetting ordeal, I looked down on her and berated her for not being macho. Why? Because the man, including this one, thinks he must always dominate the male-female situation. And since pregnancy keeps a man totally on the sidelines, completely out of control, then he must find some way to get back on top and call the shots. So, I resorted to the tactics of the playground, playing the bully. But it didn't work. Whether I liked it or not, it was up to Ellen to drink the junk. And no matter how much I scolded and complained, it didn't help.

And so it will be in the delivery room. It will be her stomach and her pain, and no matter how much tougher I am, no matter how much more pain I can endure, it means nothing. She must do the laboring. And I must prepare myself to accept that fact. I must learn that, if I am to be of any value during those grueling hours, it is as a member of the team, not the captain, but a coach, a helper, a supporter. On the sidelines, out of the spotlight, my ego in check, my male bravado out the window. In those life-and-death hours, I must convince myself of what I know is true, that the two most important people involved in the birth process are my wife and my son. Followed by the doctors, the nurses, the technicians and, somewhere in there, me. If I fail her, laboring will be both physically as well as emotionally devastating. And if I fail, she will be abandoned at the time she most needs my help and support.

Maybe I just can't get over the fact that the so-called "weaker sex" is the one whose strength and courage is ultimately tested.

September 14, 1984

Babies are smarter than people think they are.

It's often said that babies are good teachers. But now, eleven weeks before his birth, our baby prepares us for his arrival. That's putting it mildly. He's whipping us into shape. He's not so cruel as to enter the world and start screaming and fussing for food in the middle of the night. No, sir. Not our son. Far in advance of his entrance, he's making sure neither of us sleeps more than three and a half hours at a stretch. It's a charitable act, him giving us this sneak preview of what's to come.

He accomplishes this by having grown so large within his mother that he's pushing Ellen's organs out of the way.

"Jump back, small intestine! Step aside, bladder. Baby needs more room."

The result is that Ellen is extremely uncomfortable, especially when lying down. She suffers heartburn, leg cramps and must make middle-of-the-night trips to the bathroom. So, no matter how early we get to sleep, I can be sure that Ellen will stumble out of bed at 3AM and again at 8AM and make just enough noise to wake me up, too.

No one had the guts to warn me of what fatherhood promises. No one but my son, the teacher, that is, who is giving me fair warning that for the next few years I can forget about ever getting a good night's sleep.

September 25, 1984

An amazing aspect of being an expectant father is good things, unexpected things, keep happening. Before conception I would have been unable to predict that my relationship with my parents, particularly with my father, which was often quiet or removed, would now flourish as a result of Ellen's pregnancy.

Yet that is exactly what has happened. Parental conversations that once covered the normal subjects, work, weather and sports, all in a four-minute, long-distance call, have now expanded to twenty- and thirty-minute talks covering everything from politics to Pampers.

The catalyst for this strengthening of familial bonds is, of course, the baby. Their grandchild to come. The continuation of my parents' lineage, a dose of immortality. But there is more to this rush of communication, this surge of love, than their anticipation of baby pictures: a dose of grandparental pride.

My decision to have a child reaffirms their having had children. It is tangible evidence that the key decision of my parents' lives, to raise a family, was the best of all possible decisions. But more than that, this new closeness comes from a shared perspective. My parents and I now view the world from the same vantage point. That of knowing and of feeling that there is someone in life more important than ourselves. That there is someone else whose needs take priority over our own. Someone else who needs to be loved and appreciated more than we need to be loved and appreciated. Someone who is worth living for and, if necessary, worth dying for.

Having this knowledge, sharing this knowledge, puts the decades of debates and of blood feuds behind. This knowledge trivializes all the differences that have come before and suddenly seemed to have vanished. There is, as I foresee it, no more call to fight my father to satisfy my egotistic needs. No more reason to try to topple him, to prove my worth, my manhood. Now I share his view. Once a father's son, now a son's father. We have been both father and son. We have by our position, by our action, by our desire, perhaps our need to create life, come to understand one another without having to explain too much of what it is that we understand. What I now understand is what my father understood thirty years ago. It is this: that years from now my son will look at a photo of me, the proud father holding his newborn, and my boy will wonder, as I once wondered, who that man was, what he was thinking, what he was like before he got so old and so gray. His guesses will only be guesses. He will not know. Until, like his father and his father's father, he, too, becomes a father. And then the pain of not knowing one's father as a young man will no longer matter. For in that time when his wife's belly is full with the child who will make him whole, he will see, as I see now, the world from the same perspective as my father sees it, the same as his father saw it, which is how his father saw it, and his father saw it, as all fathers have seen it, as far back as there have been fathers. As a son, as a father, as a grandfather, and as a spirit that left behind a legacy of love.

VII
THE FEAR FACTOR

September 28, 1984

"Your baby is breech."

These words made me dizzy. Made Ellen cry. I sat staring at the wall, but didn't see anything. A vacuum linked my stomach to my brain. My insides emptied. My body's weight accumulated in my head. I thought, "This is what it'll feel like when I'm told my father's dead." I looked at Ellen. She looked scared. It had been a perfect pregnancy, until the doctor said those four words. Now there was worry. The doctor sensed our gloom. I sensed Ellen's disappointment. I also sensed my own fear, which was absolute. I knew that I needed information. "Is the baby in danger?" is all I could think as the doctor explained the risk factor of naturally delivering a breech baby. I tuned out the conversation. I needed one answer. "Does breech mean there is anything wrong with our baby?" The answer was no. Maybe he's breech because the umbilical is keeping him from turning head-down the way he's supposed to be. Maybe he'll still turn over, though the odds of that are only 30%. But there was no reason to think anything was wrong. But, of course, we do. We worry. Five minutes ago everything was delightfully dull—but now we worry. We can't help but do so.

It looks as though Ellen's going to have to have a Caesarean—the one thing she's dreaded. The anesthesia, the IV's, all the medical stuff, the stuff she so dislikes, may very well be part of her birthing experience. For me, this means an anxious and unhappy wife. A wife who may have to undergo surgery and its risks, spend more time in the hospital and have a tougher time recovering. It means the heavy stress begins even earlier than expected. It means a sudden loss of confidence. It means asking myself questions and thinking thoughts that until today I had the luxury of ignoring. It means a resurgence of helplessness. It means more prayers. It means everything and it means nothing. It means a loss of appetite one hour and insatiable hunger the next. It means the parental psyche, the worrier-protector, has been born within me and will remain within from now until forever.

September 29, 1984

Ellen ran into a friend at her pregnancy exercise class today whose baby was breech. Yet two weeks before the baby was due, her doctor performed a maneuver that turned the baby from head up to head down and the woman delivered naturally.

Ellen reported this story with great enthusiasm. Whereas yesterday she was agitated and gloomy, today she is excited and hopeful.

So go Ellen's moods, so go mine.

September 30, 1984

"How much are those Wibbies?"

"Which Wibbies?"

"The white Wibbies."

"The Wibbies in the window?"

"Yes, how much are those Wibbies in the window?"

I am surrounded by pregnant women talking gerbil talk and am trying to persuade Ellen to leave the madness of Fred Segal's "50% Off End of Summer Sale." But it is a losing cause.

Wibbies are marked down from $32 to $16. Likewise Absorba. And Sun & Sand and Farrel Apparel. Petit Bateau baby socks regularly $4.95 are now two pairs for that price. We'd be nuts to leave now after having waited thirty-five minutes in line just to get inside.

Inside it is packed and crazy. For a moment I think I am in a Russian market just as a shipment of grapes has arrived. But the prices affixed to a pair of socks no bigger than my thumb assure me that I am in a most capitalistic setting.

People who had shoved in line, pressing to squeeze into the store before the guard locked the door, now grab the nearest piece of merchandise, anything at all will do, hold it against their bodies, then drape the garment over their forearm for keeps or drop it on the nearest stack of clothes and push on.

Ellen can't decide which of the three Wibbies one-piece jumpsuits to buy. They are bright and colorful and any baby, especially our baby, would look adorable in them. But even at half-price they're expensive. And then I say something that I knew I shouldn't say, but I cannot keep from saying it.

"Buy them all. My son will have only the best."

Is it possible to spoil a child in utero? Heck, all this buying is for us. I know that. I mean I hardly expect to bring our infant home, open the door to his room and hear him say, "Gee, dad, you and mom did a bang-up job decorating the nursery. I feel confident I'm going to get the most out of these, my formative years."

So we buy more than we need. More than we can afford. We buy because we cannot contain our excitement. Our hope. We buy because we want to show off. Because we are proud. Because we have to do something with all this love, and since he is not here yet, it is a way of expressing that love, certainly not to the child, but maybe to ourselves or to each other.

Moments later, Ellen's inability to say "no" to Wibbies has spread to the t-shirt department, where she is unable to say "no" to button-ups and long-sleeve pullovers. And then it hits me. I'm jealous. Of my yet-to-be-born son. And I move instinctively to the men's department and run up a bill of my own. Shirts, pants, I don't need them. I know that. And I know what I am doing. I am competing. With the air. With my child who is not yet my child. The struggle has already begun. How do I pull back the reins so that we both can enjoy his life? How jealous will I feel when he's a young man discovering his potency and I am an old man dodging death? How will I love him then? When his youth frightens me, when his independence towers over me and mocks me.

I am jealous of the very life I have breathed into him. I want what he does not yet have. I want to be young again.

October 4, 1984

I am a suburbanite. I have returned to the place that I spent my youth trying to escape.

I did this voluntarily. I say I did it for my kid's sake, but surely I did it for myself. The past five years I lived in the city, surrounded by the poor, the lost, the crazed. Within that time, I have been each of those things—at one moment or another. After five years I couldn't, or wouldn't, take it anymore.

And so I moved.

It is quiet here in the suburbs. The only sounds are the white noise from the nearby freeway and the fluorescent lights' constant hum. Both sounds bypass the ear but do not escape the brain. The suburban quiet is not a soothing quiet. It is not the country's calm.

The suburban quiet is a pseudo-quiet, which is simultaneously reassuring and distressing. It feels as if no one here will do us harm. Yet it feels as if one were to try to do us harm, there would be no one here to help. There are so few people outdoors that the few people I spot, particularly at night, seem potentially dangerous. But it does feel better than where I lived yesterday.

I wonder what the suburbs, the quiet, will do to my mind, my heart. This afternoon I walked around my new neighborhood and saw only two teenaged girls jogging and a retired man mowing his lawn. No one saw me. No one saw each other. What I saw more than anything else were signs planted in front yards. They are the colorful signs of security companies that, in addition to their names, read: "Armed Patrol" or "Armed Response." Almost every yard, including ours, has one.

Very likely this is the neighborhood, or very much like the neighborhood, in which our son will be raised. Safe, quiet, a little dull. Who knows what he'll make of it. I learned just yesterday that children see the world much differently than adults.

On my old block live two brothers, George and Christian, eight and ten, immigrants from Romania. They are bright, friendly boys who stop whatever game they're playing when they see me walking my dog.

"Jester, Jester!" they cry and they smother the pup with affection. Yesterday I brought Jester by so we could all say goodbye.

Christian, the ten-year-old, asked why I was moving. I did not tell him this neighborhood terrified me. I told him we needed more room because of the baby, which is true. He was baffled. "But this is such a beautiful neighborhood. Grass, trees. Plenty of space to play. And children. It is full of children. I must have a hundred friends. And we play together all the time. This is a beautiful place to live."

I guess a neighborhood is what you make of it.

October 6, 1984

Our housekeeper, Irma, who is from Guatemala, brought her sister, Connie, with her today to work. Connie, who does baby-care work, took one long look at Ellen and whispered to Irma in Spanish, "Seven pounds, not much water."

When Irma translated what her sister had said, I was stunned. "Seven pounds, not much water" is precisely what our doctors have said.

Our doctors are charging us two thousand dollars for the same information that Connie is giving us for free. However, the M.D.s and Connie differ on one major point. Connie says we're going to have a girl.

A girl would be fine with me. It would be quite a surprise, but as long as she's healthy, I will be overjoyed. After all, a girl can wear the Mets' t-shirt and pants we've bought, same as a boy. But I think it only fair that if the doctors have erred in predicting our child's sex that they either give us a partial refund due to mental suffering we have incurred while contemplating our son's circumcision, or, at the very least, get rid of those expensive medical procedures that forecast sex and in their place hire Connie.

October 9, 1984

This morning our friend, Mimi, dropped by with her two-year-old son, Cisco. While Ellen and Mimi talked shop—pregnancy and motherhood—Cisco and I played with the toy boats and the plastic octopus that the previous tenants' children left in the back yard.

After a while it was time for a snack, and in addition to requesting apple juice, Cisco pointed into the pantry and said "Cyril." I couldn't remember purchasing anything called "Cyril" so I placed my hand on a can of sardines and said, "This?" "No." My hand moved to a can of peeled tomatoes. "No!" A jar of pet vitamins. "No." "No" to a tin of herbal tea, a package of Chinese noodles, a box of oatmeal as well as a container of sea salt. Finally my hand stopped on a bag of Oatios.

"Cyril!" Cisco said. "Cyril!"

Oatios are cereal. "Horsey food," in Cisco's words. So I poured him about fourteen chipped Oatios, which are the size and shape of Cheerios. Fourteen Oatios do not even begin to fill up the bottom of a cereal bowl.

We sat at the kitchen table and I watched Cisco eat his Oatios and drink his juice. And doing this I learned a valuable prefatherhood lesson: *Kids Eat Slowly.* Very, very slowly. I mean, fourteen chipped Oatios amount to two, maybe three spoonsful worth. It took Cisco twenty minutes to eat those fourteen Oatios. He took long pauses between each Oatio. To me, the Oatios all looked about the same.

But Cisco peered into the bowl after each swallow, studied the layout of the remaining cereal pieces and then chose which Oatio would be eaten next. It all seemed quite methodical and scientific to me.

And so when it comes time to feed my child, I will remember Cisco and the wisdom he shared with me: Don't rush a kid through dinner. It won't do a bit of good.

October 10, 1984

The Fear Factor—what could go wrong with the delivery, what could be wrong with our baby—has heightened since we were told our baby is breech. It is not only that the possibility of a Caesarean depresses and frightens us, but now that we are in the eighth month, it is time to discard some of the pleasant fantasies of being expectant parents and begin to face the reality of the coming event. This is not the fun part of the process.

After learning of the breech, we said little about it. Secretly we went to the books to research what might or might not happen if our baby remains right side up, which is really upside down. But I knew we were hiding our fears from each other when I found that all the pages in our baby books that dealt with breech and Caesarean had bent corners.

After several days of gathering knowledge in private, we admitted our concerns, compared information, then compiled the following list of questions:

If Ellen is to have a Caesarean section, will the doctors set a date or will she go into labor, report to the hospital and then be operated on?

How many days following the birth will she have to spend in the hospital?

Can I spend nights in the hospital with her?

Will the baby be able to room in or will they whisk him off to the nursery and bring him back only for feedings?

Why is Ellen's stomach blueish and sensitive?

What causes her stomach pains that feel like pin-pricks?

What about this procedure to turn the baby over so she can deliver naturally?

Will the C-section cut be a bikini cut or a long vertical cut?

The more we talked, the more we realized we were in the dark. So we typed all our questions and prepared to quiz the doctor at tomorrow's visit.

October 11, 1984

Good doctors are good therapists.

Whereas yesterday we were anxious and fearful, today we are at ease. Confident about the delivery and our baby, yet not overconfident. Our questions have been answered. Even the questions that Dr. Blanchard answered with "I don't know" now seem less ominous. Being in the presence of a knowledgeable person whom we trust makes a major difference in how we feel.

When Ellen told Dr. Blanchard that Jacqueline Snow, the nurse-practitioner, had said that the baby's chances of turning are three in ten, Dr. Blanchard said, "Caca." It doesn't seem like sound medical advice, what one learns during the grueling years of med school, but it sure made us feel good. "Caca." The baby will turn. It's early. He's got time. And to help him along, Ellen is to lie on a board set at a forty-five-degree angle twice a day when she has an empty stomach.

That's what Ellen's doing at this moment. Her head is on the ground, her legs up in the air, pillows are stuffed between her back and the slant board. She says she is uncomfortable. She says she is hungry. She says she can't possibly keep this up for twenty minutes. Then she says, "Caca." It'll all be okay.

October 12, 1984

We are taking childbirth classes because I want to be present at my child's birth. Well, part of me wants to be in the hospital room helping Ellen through the rigor of labor. And part of me wants to be in Cleveland on business.

Once again, as it is so often with this pregnancy, it is time to keep myself from running the Emotional 50-Yard Dash and face that which I would be willing to turn from. Labor and delivery. I am scared of labor and delivery and why shouldn't I be? I don't know what a contraction feels like. I don't know what it's like to battle waves of pain for eighteen or thirty consecutive hours. I don't know what it's like to pass a seven-and-a-half-pounder out of my body and when the ordeal is finally completed, I still won't know. I'll never know. Perhaps it's the knowledge of giving birth that makes women so alien to men. Perhaps having fought it out with nature and not having triumphed over nature but having become nature's partner is what makes women both intimate with physical pain and so unwilling to inflict it upon others. And perhaps it is male jealousy of women's strength, jealousy of never being put to such a test, that causes us to stumble through life trying to prove our toughness, knowing that whatever games we invent, from wrist-wrestling to nuclear war, we couldn't possibly endure what women do. I know that the two principal players in my quest for immortality, my wife and my child, could accomplish their task with or without me alongside the hospital bed. So I impose myself on this birth. I must be a player in this game.

Before we enrolled in these classes, my guess was that co-ed childbirth and Lamaze were middle-class fads perpetuated on American men by lonely, fearful women who wanted a hand to hold during labor and delivery. But after two classes I have changed my mind. The willingness of so many of us to learn these skills, to voluntarily enter the horrifying world of the labor and delivery is not only a result of our emotional awakening, but it is also for now our ultimate macho challenge.

The world of the married American man is a tame world. There are no more sexual exploits to brag about, or if there are sexual adventures, they must be concealed. So the new man, the 80's man, must find an avenue to display his courage, to show off his strength. And so we have discovered that place where our emotional battles can best be played out. The labor and delivery rooms have become our arena. It is here where we fight our latest battle. Here we test the limits of our new manhood. Can we last through labor's exhausting hours? Can we tolerate not being in charge? Not being the center of attention? And if we do succeed beyond labor, how much more can we endure? Can we watch the episiotomy? Can we watch as the baby comes out? Where will our eyes focus when the placenta appears?

Oddly enough, today's test of manhood has wound up in the one place that until recently no one who called himself a real man would have ever dreamed of looking.

October 18, 1984

For the fourth consecutive night, Ellen sleeps away from home. For the fourth consecutive night, I lay in an empty bed.

We are not quarrelling. We are polyurethaning. The fumes are heavy, dangerous to pregnant mother and child. So Ellen sleeps at a friend's home.

After dropping Ellen off, I drove on Wilshire Boulevard, passing several singles' bars. As a red light I watched a college couple necking beneath a blinking neon sign that read "Cocktails." For a moment I thought about parking and going inside. I wondered if at my advanced age of thirty-three any women at the bar would find me intriguing enough to talk to. Attractive enough to take home. I drove home alone, where I munched on everything that was munchable. I watched David Letterman, then showered until all the hot water was gone. At 3 A.M. I went to bed thinking. Thinking about women who are not my wife. As the pregnancy continues, these thoughts, often erotic, become more frequent. I recalled my bachelor days from Hollywood all the way back to high school. One by one I thought of each woman I fell in love with or thought I had. One by one I tried to imagine what my life would be like had I married one of my ex-girlfriends instead of Ellen. Where would I live now? What kind of work would I do? Could I already have children? Be divorced?

I envisioned them as the young women they were, for that is how I remember them. Judy was voluptuous but silly. Sandy I hardly knew. Diane was too religious. Katie's serving time. Leslie died at 29.

Tonight has been a lonely night. The kind of night that makes me think that a lasting, hard-fought love is better than an uncommitted passion. Though the desire for such passion never disappears.

Tonight reminds me of all the choices, all the compromises I've made along the way. It makes me think that to a large degree I've done with my life pretty much what I wanted to do. Oh, I'm not rich or famous like I had planned to be. And I certainly won't accomplish a fraction of what I set out to do. I foresee years and years of struggle ahead just to meet the bills. I don't know if I'll ever own a home.

But something subtle, subconscious, led me to where I am, obviously to where I wanted to go. Committed to a relationship, expecting a child, accepting the responsibilities that come with it. I sit here, the almost-father, philosophizing in my present idealized state. I feel proud. Smart. Successful. But I wonder.

Two months from now, when my thoughts are interrupted by an exasperated woman demanding I either change my son's diaper or file for divorce, I wonder if I'll feel so confident about all those decisions that brought me to where I am.

October 20, 1984

A television commercial of the near future:

EXT. OREGON WILDERNESS—NIGHT

We see a log cabin. The CAMERA MOVES CLOSER and CLOSER until we are at the cabin's window looking inside.

INT. LOG CABIN—NIGHT

Four guys on loan from Gentlemen's Quarterly sit around a poker table drinking beer, munching chips and studying their cards. A fireplace blazes behind them. Their rifles rest against the wall beneath a mounted moose head. We are to assume they are relaxing after a long day's hunt.

One by one they toss poker chips into the pot, each matching the other.

> GUY #4
> (Tom Selleck look-alike)
> What do you say, Bobby?

> GUY #1
> (John Travolta look-alike)
> Well, I've given it a lot of thought, and when Cindy goes into labor, dammit, I'm going to be in that delivery room helping her as best I can.

Guy #1 looks around the table. We see that he is expecting a sign of approval. What he gets instead is:

GUY #2
(Jan-Michael Vincent look-alike)
Well, that's just fine, Bobby. But not only am I going to be in the delivery room when Paula gives birth, but when our little one comes out, I'm going to clip the umbilical cord. It's my special way of welcoming our child into the family of man.

Guy #2 looks at his cronies. Only Guy #1 is impressed. Guy #3 (Bubba Smith look-alike) stares at Guy #2.

GUY #3
I hate to steal your thunder, Eric, but I'm delivering our baby.
(He takes a beat for emphasis.)

At home.

Guy #1 and Guy #2 nod approvingly. Guy #4 folds his cards and lays them face down on the table.

GUY #4
Yeah, well, I'm breast-feeding.

The others stare in awe. They simultaneously lift their cans of beer and toast the Tom Selleck look-alike.

                    GUY #1
To Tom.

                    GUY #2
To Tom.

                    GUY #3
To Tom.

Guy #4 raises his beer can.

                    GUY #4
                (from the heart)
You know something? You guys are not only expectant fathers, you're good friends . . . and
beautiful people.

They clink beer cans again. The CAMERA GOES IN
TIGHT on one beer can. The label reads: "NEW MAN."
THEME MUSIC comes up.

                ANNOUNCER (V.O.)
Whenever words aren't enough, reach for New
Man. A sensitive beer for those very sensitive
times.

THEME MUSIC grows softer as we:

                FADE TO BLACK.

October 24, 1984

The baby is still breech. Jacqueline's statistic, 30% chance of turning, seems to hold. Karen's "Caca " remark may have been a placebo.

As Jacqueline examined Ellen this afternoon, she asked if we knew about the turning procedure, the manipulation that puts the baby upside down as he should be. Ellen said we had talked to Karen about it. And then Jacqueline said something to the effect that, "Then you know how Karen feels about it?" Implying, I assumed, that Karen didn't think that turning the baby was a great idea. When Ellen said that Karen seemed to be totally in favor of trying the inversion procedure, Jacqueline suddenly shifted course. Now she seemed to be saying that Karen probably felt better about the procedure these days, because of some of the muscle-relaxing drugs available that help the uterus relax and lessen the danger to mother and child. What I heard bothered me. Either I was completely misunderstanding this conversation or doctor and nurse-practitioner were not in sync about this procedure.

I asked, "Is there any danger to the baby in this procedure?"

Yes, there is some danger. But the risks are low. However, it is possible that the procedure could send the baby into distress and an emergency C-section, called a crash section, would have to be performed. But this clinic has never had to perform such an operation.

I have great faith in all the Women's Medical Group staff. If I had to pick a number on the faith meter, I'd rate them a 9.9 out of ten. I know they wouldn't take any unnecessary chances. I know that the doctors who are trained to manipulate the baby have the option of quitting at any time during the procedure if it's not working. If know they have the best monitoring equipment ever invented. I know this procedure is over one hundred years old. I know that the odds of harming our baby are very slight. But I also know that something deep inside me is troubled by the possibility of Ellen undergoing this procedure.

October 25, 1984

Now that I am a married man, an expectant father, a suburbanite and in debt, people I don't know, companies who once refused my business, now send me credit cards.

Now that I am out of the inner city, out of work and out of cash, I can put everything I want but can't afford on a piece of plastic. So this morning, Ellen and I bought baby's changing table, baby's mobile and baby's crib bumpers and put them all on our MasterCard.

After hours of comparative shopping, we were famished, so on the way home we stopped at a fairly expensive restaurant and charged our meal to MasterCard.

This evening, Ellen was looking through a baby catalog and decided to send off for a baby's first-year calendar. This, too, we charged to our new friend, MasterCard.

I just finished totalling today's expenditures. I am shocked how much money two people can spend in one day without leaving the city limits.

And then, while contemplating our enormous expenditures, I had a brainstorm.

If the MasterCard bill comes due and we can't pay it, we'll just charge it to American Express.

October 27, 1984

Since we moved into our new apartment, passing baby's room has always been depressing. Depressing because except for the Japanese lantern that covers the 100-watt ceiling bulb, his room is completely empty. An empty room is a sad room.

So yesterday we bought bookshelves. These unassembled shelves came with a page of wordless instructions. The instructions were divided into two pictures. Picture A showed all the unassembled pieces lying side by side. Picture B showed these same pieces magically assembled into the finished product. My job is to figure out how Picture A got to be Picture B.

At birth, when they passed out mechanical ability, I was obviously asleep in the nursery. I have no idea what it is that people do with pliers, screwdrivers and power tools. But with a child on the way, all that changes. Tonight, I assembled the bookshelves. In less than an hour. True, it doesn't rank with the parting of the Red Sea, but for me it was a major accomplishment.

When Ellen asked how I suddenly gained this mechanical know-how, I said, "Hey, this is for our child."

We put a teddy bear and a stuffed frog on the top shelf. Our fifteen baby-related books on the bottom shelf. In between, we found room for a softball, a multicolored abacus, Groucho glasses, a papier-mache penguin, and an Empire State Building night light. Finally, it was time to inflate the world globe.

Over and over I blew into it, but it didn't inflate. I filled my lungs and exhaled til I thought my kidneys would burst. But the world remained flat. Ellen said, "Maybe you should take it to the filling station and have them pump it up." I ignored that and tried again.

Moments later the Earth was inflated and spinning effortlessly on its axis.

Though the room is not full, it is alive. Alive with shapes and colors and textures. I asked myself why I feel such happiness as I sit here rocking in my rocker, staring at these common objects. Maybe it's because the abacus' colors are visually pleasing. Or maybe it's because as a child I had an affinity for teddy bears and having a child will give me an excuse to play with them again. But after more rocking, the answer came. I see my son's future in these objects.

He will cuddle the teddy and know that it is soft and good to touch. And not long after that I will roll the ball to him and he will stop it and roll it back. Soon after, he'll point to the abacus and say "red" or "green" or "brown." And in time he will count on it from one to ten. Later, we will play catch with the same ball. And about that time, he will be able go look at the globe and show me where he lives and where his grandparents live. He will name the names of the countries where his great-grandparents were born. And then there will come a day when he opens one of those books and reads. He will read and he will understand things without my explaining them to him. And then he will be on his way to discovering the world, to discovering himself and finding out where he fits into it—which I suppose is a lifelong pursuit.

But for now I will put down my pencil, put away my thoughts and simply stare at the objects in his bookshelves. For looking at these shapes, these colors, these textures allows me to anticipate the joy I hope will come.

October 30, 1984

Random thoughts on a Tuesday afternoon:

All expectant fathers share two concerns: "Will I be able to afford all this?" and "Is my wife's stomach going to explode?"

Ellen has gone from 108 pounds to her current weight, 134 pounds. This makes her the largest woman I've ever gone out with.

Within 30 seconds I saw the following on TV:

First, a report on the Ethiopian famine showed mothers brushing mosquitos off their dying babies. Then, on another station, I saw a robust bouncing American baby modeling Cabbage Patch designer diapers.

Designer diapers. Dying babies.

Our child is being born into a perverse world. I'm not sure how I'm going to explain it to him.

November 1, 1984

Sooner or later they had to be dealt with: diapers.

This afternoon, while Ellen was out, ABC Diaper Service solicited our business. ABC will deliver ninety, one-hundred-percent-cotton diapers once a week for $9.20 per week.

Before ABC called, I knew practically nothing about diapers. After hearing their ten-minute diaper rap, I feel like I could sell them. But of all the information ABC fed me, one statistic is unforgettable—ninety diapers a week. Ninety diapers a week come to over twelve diaper changes per day, which comes to one clean diaper every two hours.

As so often is the case with this pregnancy, I have my pocket calculator in hand. Ninety diapers at $9.20 per week comes to about 4,300 diapers per year, costing almost $500. Over a period of two and a half years, this comes to approximately 11,000 diaper changes, costing about $1,300.

And whether we have full-time help, part-time help or no help, there is no way I'll escape my share of diaper changing. I estimate that I'm looking ahead to no fewer than 3,200 diaper changes.

I have fantasized many wonderful moments since learning I would be a father. I have also fantasized moments of trauma, times of grief. But never in my visions of fatherhood have I fantasized reality. The reality of thirty-two hundred icky, dirty diapers.

On the bright side, it is thirty-two hundred private sessions with my son when I can sing to him, hold him, try to make him laugh, try to . . . .

Oh, hell, it's thirty-two hundred dirty diapers. I'll learn to live with it.

November 4, 1984

A typical day in the ninth month of pregnancy:

We are trying to determine if Ellen's and my blood types are the same. If so, I will donate blood in case she needs a transfusion during delivery.

To find the answer, I sit in the lab area of the Women's Medical Group with my shirt sleeve rolled up and my eyes averted from the needle that Yolanda, the nurse, slides into my vein.

As Ellen stands beside me saying, "Remember your Lamaze. Breathe deep and relax. Breathe deep and relax," several doctors and nurses, puzzled by my presence, stop and stare. Dr. Blanchard cannot resist.

"Yolanda, is this a pregnancy test?"

"I'm afraid it is."

"This'll make a terrific article for a medical journal. Please bring me the results."

Everyone laughs and moves on.

Moments later, we are on our way to interview a pro-spective pediatrician. We arrive early and decide to treat ourselves to ice cream cones. We are licking scoops of chocolate chip and maple walnut ice cream as we walk toward the pediatrician's office. There, we read the sign outside his office:

Dr. M.L. Johnson
Pediatrics
Pediatric Nutrition

Ellen speaks first.

"I can't go in there eating an ice cream cone. How would it look? His specialty is nutrition."

"Not good, considering our first question is, 'How do we keep our child from eating sugar?'"

"Maybe we should throw away our cones."

"Maybe we should just eat them very quickly."

Which is what we do before entering his office.

Sitting on the waiting room sofa, I practice my introductory remarks:

"We're looking for a doctor whose nutritional views meet with ours. We believe our baby's diet should exclude formula, store-bought baby food, red meat, junk food and anything with sugar."

Perhaps I should also add that we're looking for a doctor whose views on nutrition are less hypocritical than ours.

November 9, 1984

I love show biz.

When we're down to our last $200 and the rent's due at the end of the week, we can pound on studio doors, call every producer we know, plead with our agents to help us find work and we'll strike out. But when work is the furthest thing from our minds, when we're close to becoming parents and there is much to be done before baby's arrival, Hollywood calls.

At 9:15 this evening, Friday night, the phone rang. It was our agent.

"Great news. I got a call from Universal's Business Affairs office. They want to negotiate a contract—immediately."

"With us?"

"Yes, with you."

I tried to remember the last time we had contact with anyone at Universal Studios. I drew a blank.

"What's this concern?"

"You're the new head writers for the TV show BURTON LOVES BAMBI."

"We are?"

"This is a tremendous break for your careers. BURTON LOVES BAMBI is a class act. Everyone in the industry respects the hell out of it. Congratulations."

"Jerry, I've got to slow you down for a second. Seeing as how we've never been interviewed for this job, since we never even knew this job existed, it strikes me as odd that we've suddenly been hired."

"What can I say? They read your work. They think you're talented. And they can't wait for the two of you to get on board."

"We're not saying 'yes.' We're not saying 'no.' But Ellen and I have this little quirk—we like to meet the person who hires us before going to work for him. We've never even met anyone involved with BURTON LOVES BAMBI which I believe ranked sixty-fifth last week out of sixty-six prime time shows. Be honest, Jerry, they're dying, aren't they?"

"All I can tell you is that Sid Rose is the producer. And trust me on this one. He's a class act. Everyone in the industry respects the hell out of him. We represent him. And he wants you two on the set Monday morning at ten."

"Ellen checks into the hospital Monday morning at eight for a medical procedure."

"How long will she be on the table?"

"We should be finished by eleven."

"Then you'll go in after lunch. I'll smooth it out with Sid. Besides, I need time to negotiate with Business Affairs. So what do you say? Isn't it just what the doctor ordered?"

"Ellen and I'll talk it over and call you back tomorrow morning."

"Hey, no rush. Call me first thing Monday morning."

"We can call you tomorrow."

"Skiing in Big Bear over the weekend. Call me Monday. And think about how much money you want."

"We'd like $25,000 a week."

"Think a lot lower and have a beautiful weekend. And congratulations again. This is the break that's going to turn it all around for you . . . . Oh, one last thing. There's a strong possibility that BURTON LOVES BAMBI will be cancelled in three weeks. So they can only guarantee you a 21-day contract. When's the baby due?"

"In 22 days."

"Then it's perfect! Talk to you Monday. And think numbers. Goodbye."

This job requires we work from 10AM to midnight Monday through Friday. If there was a medical emergency we'd be twenty miles from the hospital. In traffic it could take over an hour to get there. Plus, every Wednesday at 11 AM (between now and due date) Ellen has a doctor's appointment. She couldn't work those mornings. We have four interviews lined up with potential baby-care helpers. We haven't solved the diaper dilemma.

A baby is born once in a lifetime. We can always get another job.

But I don't think Jerry will understand.

VIII
TURN OR BE TURNED

November 12, 1984

Our baby turned his first somersault.

After Ellen was hooked up to an IV that pumped a muscle relaxant into her body, Dr. Katie Moyer and Dr. Patricia Robertson, whose combined weight is far less than that of an average NFL linebacker, using only their hands, manipulated the contents of Ellen's stomach in such a way that our baby, who had been head up for as long as we can remember, is now head down and in the proper position for a vaginal delivery.

The actual procedure, called an External Version, took about twelve minutes. I sat beside Ellen, looking into her eyes and trying to help her concentrate on her breathing while the doctors provided our son with a new view of the world.

Occasionally I forced myself to peek over my shoulder to check out the goings-on. Surprisingly it was not scary. But strange to see Ellen's stomach changing shape as if it were a water-filled Baggie that indented with every ounce of pressure. Though Ellen felt discomfort, only once did she cry out in pain.

And then it was over and the certainty of a Caesarean was reduced to a possibility of Caesarean, depending on what happens during labor and delivery. But for now, we can at least hope for a normal birth.

Though External Version took only minutes, Ellen was in the hospital bed from 8AM to 8PM undergoing monitoring and tests to make sure the baby was okay before, during and after the procedure.

For the moment he seems to be fine.

November 13, 1984

And now a few words about circumcision.

According to some doctors with whom I've spoken, circumcision is not a medical necessity. Despite popular medical opinion, the overwhelming majority of baby boys born in America are circumcised. In addition, all Jewish and Moslem baby boys, according to religious law, must be circumcised.

Since I am not willing to fight 5,000 years of tradition, I now find myself interviewing "mohels," the religious Jews who perform the circumcision rite, which they do in the parents' home. I can hardly wait.

To prepare myself for what to expect when it is our turn to host this strange event, I attended such a ceremony, known as a "bris," this morning. It was the first one I had ever witnessed. Other than my own, which, believe me, I don't remember.

Well, there were about a dozen guests gathered at our friends', Lonnie and Julie's, home for their son's bris. The ceremony, blessings and all, takes about six minutes. But I was conscious for only the first three minutes, for after the mohel made the cut, I fainted.

I slid against Ellen's body and crashed to the hardwood floor. On the way down, my head hit a table, which caromed into the wall. Meanwhile, the ceremony continued un-interrupted as the infant's mother administered an ice pack to my neck and the infant's aunt consoled Ellen, who, upon noticing that my eyeballs had rolled up into my head and my lips were white, screamed, thinking I was dead.

Within minutes I recovered, more embarrassed than hurt, apologized for my behavior, downed some orange juice, said my goodbyes, then drove home, seriously considering the possibility of becoming Baptist for the month of December.

November 14, 1984
2:05PM

It's getting close. Real close. The baby could arrive in six hours or six days.

This morning, Dr. Blanchard examined Ellen and said, "You're three centimeters dilated." Four to five centimeters is when the contractions start really hurting and some women want pain relief. Ten centimeters means labor is almost over, the woman has gone through hell and now it's time to push out the baby.

Good God! Even as I write, Ellen, who is lying on the sofa reading, just went "Ooh, I'm feeling cramps." It could be any second. Now is no time for me to walk the dog for an hour or call Davey, or Bryan and ask if they want to play racquetball this evening. From now til we're at the hospital, I'm going to make sure I know where Ellen is every moment.

During this morning's examination, Dr. Blanchard felt the baby's head. I was jealous. Someone else made contact, touched our baby first. But I was delighted to hear that the umbilical was not a threat, not wrapped around his neck. He's in the birth canal, head down, right where he's supposed to be.

November 14, 1984
3:55PM

Returned from pharmacy with rubbing alcohol, cotton swabs, indoor thermometer and our first box of infant diapers. We're ready.

November 14, 1984
4:10PM

Ellen says she's having premenstrual-like cramps. She checked a book. It's a sign of oncoming labor.

November 14, 1984
4:20PM

Ellen's suitcase, washcloths, lip chap, cassette records and tapes, pens, notebooks, magazine, toothbrush, toothpaste, receiving blanket, baby clothes and medical file are packed and in the car. Things she still needs, bathrobe, nightgown, telephone book, pillows and slippers, will be thrown in the trunk minutes before we head toward the hospital.

November 14, 1984
4:45PM

I'm hoping the baby waits at least til tomorrow morning. Neither Ellen nor I slept well last night and we'd both like to be well-rested when we confront labor.

It would be great if we could take a nap now, but we're on our way to see the kingpin agent at our agency, who is angry at us for not taking the BURTON LOVES BAMBI job.

November 14, 1984
4:52PM

Terry Hughes, who is a director-producer at Warner Brothers, just called to set up a Friday afternoon meeting. He is directing the Showtime TV series STEAMBATH and wants us to write an episode.

Because we like Terry and want to work with him, we set a Friday date and promised to be there, ready to work. But I'm not sure we can make that meeting.

November 15, 1984
3:02AM

I am a father.

I have been such a person since 9:55 last night when I witnessed creation. Either the first moment of it. Or the end result. Whichever, it has not yet sunk in.

I sit home alone. My wife and my son share a hospital room. Exhausted from their struggle, they try to sleep. Our son succeeds. Ellen does not. Ellen can only look at the baby and not quite believe it is hers. Though holding him, she says, "seems the most natural thing in the world."

He came seventeen days early. He checked in light, five pounds, fourteen ounces. They say he looks exactly like me. I only recognize the nose. He appears to be perfectly healthy. As does his mom.

After listening to our agent philosophize from 5:20 to 6:40, mostly about our inability to make him wealthy, we came home and ate. At 7:30 we drove to Santa Monica to our bimonthly religious studies group. In this group, we struggle with theological and moral questions and try to explore what the Bible and prayer mean in our daily lives.

At 7:50 we were assembled, mingling and munching crackers and cheese. At 8:10 our studies began. Tonight's discussion began with Genesis 2:1-4, the verses concerning the Sabbath Day. At 8:35 Ellen leaned over and suggested we go home. But our friends, Lotus and Emily, told us to call the doctor. Then another friend, Sara, who recently gave birth, advised us to go straight to the hospital. We called and Dr. Katie Moyer told Ellen that if it would make Ellen feel better, she'd meet her right away at the hospital.

As we exited the building's lobby, Ellen grabbed a handrail and buckled to the floor. A contraction first seized, then paralyzed her. Several deep breaths later, she made it to the car.

The drive to the hospital was murderous. Ellen's contractions were six minutes apart and they were nasty. I tried to take her mind off her pain by counting down the blocks to the hospital. We arrived at the hospital entrance at the stroke of 9, the same time as Dr. Moyer.

Ellen was put in a wheelchair and taken to the labor room as I signed forms and handed over our Blue Cross cards, which checked us in.

What happened next happened quickly. Ellen was dilated to four and her contractions were vicious. She tried breathing through them, but sometimes she was too tense to do so. I stood beside her watching as her body flinched violently and seemed to throw itself backward against the bed. It looked like a scene out of "THE EXORCIST."

Through it all she cried out in pain. And when she was not screaming, she was on her side, pressing against me, her nails clawing into my shoulders.

Her water broke. She vomited. She gushed blood. She begged for pain relief. The nurse prepared to examine Ellen, saying, "Let's see where you are and then if Dr. Moyer thinks it's okay, we'll give you medication."

And then I read trouble in the nurse's eyes. As Ellen pleaded for drugs, the nurses scrambled.

"Dr. Moyer! Stat! Dr. Moyer! Stat!"

The nurses disappeared, then quickly re-entered, wheeling a blue metal file box.

"Please give me relief!" Ellen cried.

"We can't," the nurse said. "You're about to have a baby!"

"Please. For the pain."

"It's too late. Your baby's coming!" It was 9:44. Labor was supposed to last six, twelve, thirty hours. Not forty-four minutes.

The nurses set up. One seemed preoccupied with Dr. Moyer's whereabouts. Then it hit me. The nurses were panicked that they were going to have to deliver our baby.

I was there for all of this. I watched my wife suffer, bleed, curse and cry. There was no time to daydream. No excuse to leave, much as I wanted to. I remembered our Lamaze instructor's advice. Empathize, talk to your wife. Tell her you know it hurts. Tell her you care. This is what I tried to do. Was I successful? Unsuccessful? I don't know. All I knew is that if I had missed this evening, I would have missed the most extraordinary moments of my life.

The baby was coming. It was time for Ellen to push. Hold her breath and push. She was having trouble.

"Your baby's head is right here. See it, Dennis?" Dr. Moyer said. "Push, Ellen. Take a deep breath, hold it and push."

I held one of Ellen's legs back. The nurse held back the other. It wasn't working. Ellen was overly tense.

"Give her oxygen."

The nurse slipped an oxygen mask over Ellen's nose and mouth. Ellen would have none of it. She ripped it off and flung it in the nurse's face.

"Push. Deep breath and push! Good. Again. Deep breath, lean on the air, tuck your chin and push."

And then.

"On your next contraction," Katie said, "you're going to have a baby."

The idea of not looking was impossible. Ellen took a deep breath, pressed, pushed. Again, deep breath, pressure, push!

And then, the back of the head! A bloody balloon swelling between her legs. And in an instant, the shoulders, dripping with blood, rose perpendicular to the bed, like a whale breaching out of the water. And then a whole baby. Our baby. A dark-red, almost purplish baby, still connected to the cord, which, too, was dark red, purplish.

Towels draped and dried the baby. And then he was on his mother's breast. They say he cried, but I don't remember hearing him.

I remember kissing Ellen's forehead, remember leaning over to kiss Katie. I peeked at my boy hidden in those towels. I didn't get it. It was 9:55. And it was all over.

He is healthy. I put my finger to his hand and he grasped it. He is my son. I had witnessed his birth. And it all seemed so normal. Now it was over. Ellen's pain was gone. She held her son. I stroked her forehead. The pregnancy. This cherished pregnancy was over. And those final moments seemed so perfectly goddamn normal.

Katie clamped the umbilical cord. Would I like to clip it? Not really. But then I took the instrument and clipped. No possibility of my becoming a surgeon. It took me two clips to cut through it.

I attacked the pay phone. My parents, Ellen's parents. The study group that was just breaking up. As Emily announced it, I heard their shock, then their cry of exultation in the background. I called friends in town. Friends in the

Midwest. In the East. I cared nothing about waking people up.

At 2:05 I kissed Ellen and my son goodbye. We are lucky. Whoever heard of a fifty-five-minute labor? The thought of what might have happened had Sara not advised us to go straight to the hospital still terrifies me. The baby might have beat the doctor to the hospital. I might have had to deliver the boy at home.

Now there are a million thoughts. The circuits cannot carry them all at once. When the nurse asked me to name our pediatrician, I froze. We had not made our final decision. I answered anyway. Dr. Sachs. Yesterday we interviewed Dr. Marshall Sachs. We liked him alot. Days before, we met with another pediatrician we also liked. All things being equal, I think I made the choice based on the fact that Dr. Sachs has a more convenient parking lot than his competitor.

My son, like all babies, is heavenly and gorgeous. Thinking of him makes me cry. Already I cannot stand being away from him. I drove home on the desolate L.A. streets, thinking "drive slowly." Now I have to be careful not only for my own safety, but I must be around for a little boy who needs a father today and hopefully for a long time to come.

November 15, 1984
5:48AM

A final thought before going to bed:

When I was sixteen and a half, I could not be convinced that there was a God. Now that I am twice that age and have held my son who will one day talk back to me, I could not be convinced that there is not a God.

I cannot explain why good people die young, why children die before they have time to contemplate their own existence. I don't know why so many shitty people have it better than so many decent ones.

But I know if you walk into a hospital with a pregnant woman and you believe in nothing, that if you leave that hospital with that same woman and her baby, you'll damn well believe in something.

IX
BEYOND BIRTH

November 15, 1984
5:02PM

With the new life come new rhythms. Or perhaps I should say no rhythms. The day is divided into phone calls, meals eaten on the run, visitors who've come to see the baby, trips from hospital to home to walk the dog.

The new life brings new thoughts, new perceptions of the world.

Why don't men take paternity leaves? Why is time off, if any, basically reserved for women? Why don't we take a month off. In those first few chaotic days, filled with ecstasy and fear, the family needs to be together. Being together in times of joy and sadness is what a family is. A month's distance from the office grind, from the bottom line could not help but create a healthier world.

Ellen began the day sharing a room with a couple whose baby is suffering brain damage. The nursing staff transferred Ellen to a different room. Why make the grieving parents suffer more at the sight of a jubilant family? Why make the jubilant parents suppress their natural feelings? It was a most-uncomfortable situation. All that separated life's ultimate triumph from life's ultimate despair was a thin cloth divider. There was no gesture, no word of comfort that could bridge that unjust gap.

It is said that when a man has his first son it is a sign of virility. Yet, as I stood next to Dr. Sachs this morning, listening to him describe what might have to be done to our boy in case he suffered from an intestinal obstruction—x-rays, intravenous feedings, tubes probing from his mouth down to his stomach—I felt not manly but powerless. If my son was seriously ill, I could not save him. At best I could sit on the sidelines and pay another man who might be able to help.

Babies reinforce the need for community. In the past thirty hours I have needed the help of two doctors, at least a dozen nurses, countless hospital administrators, a pharmacy clerk, a hardware store salesman, a professional cook, two handymen and a lot of friends just to prepare for bringing our baby home.

I had this vision. It is Sunday and the streets are quiet. Ellen and I bring our baby home. We introduce him to our cats and dog. We show baby around the house where he will soon learn to crawl and walk. We change his clothes, place him in the bassinet and watch him sleep. Then we turn to each other and say, "Now what?"

November 15, 1984
7:20PM

When I was a boy, old people, adults, would look at me and say something incredibly dumb like, "He's got his daddy's chin," or "his mother's eyes." I wanted to say, "Hey, stupid. These are my eyes. My chin."

This morning I heard myself say, "He's got my hair and those are definitely my eyes."

I retroactively apologize to all those old people . . . who were then probably the age that I am now.

My aunt Lily, who is in her midseventies, having lost a bout to brain cancer some time ago, lost her sight.

Despite a host of other illnesses that continue to plague her, she carries on, survives, due to her determination to live. "There are things I still want to live to do," she says.

She called tonight and congratulated me. She related a story about the first time she gave birth. It was a funny tale. On the drive to the hospital, she suffered a contraction and grabbed for the steering wheel to brace herself. In the process, she almost drove her husband and herself into a ditch.

In seriousness, she spoke of family. Of her two sons. her daughter, her eleven grandkids. There was something particularly poignant about a woman whose pain is great, whose vision is gone, taking the time to pass on the wisdom of her life to one who has so much more of life to look forward to. She ended our conversation with one simple line. She said, "Family. That's what it's all about."

I have a feeling she's right

November 16, 1984
1:15AM

Career vs. Family.

If you don't want children, don't have them. It's perfectly acceptable to refrain. No excuses necessary. There are too many people as it is anyway.

Since I do not have an outstanding career, but only a modest one, I do not know what it is to be at the top of the heap. To be full of power and money. To have people approach me with caution, to look upon me with awe. So I cannot say career is better than family. Or family is the ultimate joy. I do know that in the months I have contemplated our boy's arrival, and in the twenty-six hours since he showed up, I have grown closer to my parents, to my God, to my wife and to myself.

I cannot help but think that having chosen to sidestep pure ambition in favor of family and career, our lives will improve and our careers will soar.

Of course, I could be wrong.

November 16, 1984
10:20AM

The first thing I saw as I entered Ellen's hospital room this morning was a baby suckling at his mother's breast. It is a powerful sight.

I asked Ellen what it was like. She said, "It's like being at one with the little guy. It's so close. I don't know where my body ends and his begins. And he needs me so much. It's the ultimate seduction. I can't resist him. The moment he reaches for me, I'm hooked."

I am envious of that mother-child closeness. Their relationship is so natural. If I am to make a positive dent in this boy's life, I'm going to have to work at it. This became evident when Ellen handed me a bottle of sterilized water.

"Here. Feed him."

I held my son in the crook of my arm and when he drank from the bottle, love rippled through my body. But a moment later, he not only wanted more, but he wanted the real thing. He grabbed at my chest, was disappointed. He cried for his mother. I handed my son over. It is she who has the power.

Since we men are unable to successfully compete for the love of our infants, we run from the hospital rooms into the world of commerce, into the world of money and power, status and prestige. Here, all qualities associated with the fragility and mystery of new life being threatening are immediately crushed. The maternal instinct, the need to nurture, to love and be loved, are laughed at, despised. Affection is weakness. Kindness is suspect. Honesty feared.

The further from these feelings a man travels, the more of a man he is mistakenly considered to be. If only we were not so afraid of what it is we truly want. Not that our children admire us, nor fear us. But only that they love us.

November 17, 1984

I woke at ten, after eight luxurious hours of sleep. I got in the car and drove the speed limit or a little better all the way to the hospital. Door to door, the trip is 5.6 miles. I made it there in nine minutes.

Inside the hospital, I immediately fell prey to a baby photo opportunity and agreed to pay twenty-six dollars and some cents for ten pictures of our son.

This was followed by four trips from Ellen's room to the car to load the trunk with flowers, clothes, books and a baby blanket that I stole from the nursery.

A nurse came by and showed us how to "top and tail" baby, since we're not supposed to bathe him til the umbilical cord has healed. Then she helped Ellen dress and swaddle the baby.

Somewhere amidst all this, we were handed his birth certificate, which I was surprised to see had no footprints. Plus, we were given a bottle of complimentary champagne whose label read, "To Celebrate the Birth of your Child. Santa Monica Medical Center—Extra Dry."

A nice gesture, but I don't think I'll be serving it to guests. And finally, right before Ellen with baby cradled in her arms was seated in a wheelchair and rolled out of the hospital (standard procedure), we were given a "gift pack" that included four infant Pampers, miniature Johnson & Johnson shampoo, baby powder and lots of coupons for twenty cents off things that babies don't need but parents feel they must buy.

And then baby was strapped into his infant car seat and with Ellen sitting beside him, we drove home. Cautiously.

This time I took the city streets rather than risking our lives on the California freeways.

Those same 5.6 miles I had driven earlier in only nine minutes now took half an hour. And I drove all the way home without once changing lanes.

At home Ellen preceded me up the stairs and greeted Jester with a rawhide bone. The last thing we want is a jealous dog. I followed, carrying our baby. Jester, chewing madly on her bone, did not notice the new tenant. Nor did the cats seem to care.

We took our son to our bedroom and placed him on our bed. We could not believe what was happening to us. Or rather, what had happened to us. It was too wonderful. Too new.

"There's a prayer I've been waiting a long time to say," I told Ellen. She knew exactly what I meant. There's a prayer within our faith said not only at special times, but at special times that are also first times. It can be said when one witnesses the first snow in winter or the first blossoms of spring. It can be said the first time one tastes a pomegranate or the first time one travels abroad. It can be said when Tom Seaver throws out the first pitch of the new baseball season, or, in our case, the first time the three of us were at home. Together. A family.

I put my arm around Ellen and drew her to me. We recited the prayer first in Hebrew, then translated into English:

"Blessed Art Thou Lord Our God,
Creator of the Universe Who Has
Kept us in Life, Sustained us and
Allowed us to Reach this Wondrous Moment."

We looked at each other, then at our baby. We embraced. We kissed. And then, of course, we cried.

November 22, 1984
Thanksgiving Day

Ellen and I wrote this letter and read it to our son at his naming.

Dear Jesse Max:

Dennis: You took us by surprise.

You did not wait for your due date. Nor for your room to be completed. You barely waited for the doctor.

We sense that you like things done quickly, so we'll keep our letter short.

You have been named Jesse after two spiritual men. My uncle, Rabbi Jacob Danziger, and my dear friend, the Reverend James P. Clements.

Ellen: You have been named Max after two practical men, my grandfathers, Max Schindler and Max Izen. We hope you find a balance between the mystical and the real.

Dennis: Jesse means "gift of God." Max means "greatest." And that is what you are to us: God's greatest gift. Your Hebrew name is Yaakov Moshe.

Ellen: But you still have more names. Four or five years from now, you will come home from school and complain that when the teacher told everyone to write his name on top of the page, it took you longer than almost everyone else. But there is a reason for this.

Dennis: Moments after you were born, we realized we had not settled on your last name. But having witnessed Ellen give birth, the idea of laying sole claim to you became immediately unacceptable.

I could not erase your mother's nine months of uncertainty. Her countless hours on the cold examining room table. I could not deny her the victory she won in the labor room by branding you my own.

So you will go through life carrying both our names.

Ellen: In the short time you have been with us, you have taught us many things.

Witnessing your birth has taught us to believe in miracles.

Holding you in our arms has taught us that there is a depth to our emotions and to our love that we did not know existed.

Being with you from morning til night has taught us we can get along on four hours of sleep.

Dennis: At moments during the day we cry for no reason other than that you are now with us. We love you and pray that you have a long and healthy life. And we hope that one day you have a child of your own so that you may know how much we love you.

Love,

Mom and Dad

POSTSCRIPT

On July 15, 1986, Ellen gave birth to Molly Bess Sandler Danziger. Two days later, our daughter, who weighed 7 lbs. 5-1/2 oz. and was 20 inches long at birth (despite arriving three weeks early), came home. Mother and baby are in good health and Jesse Max, who is now 20 months, is, for the moment, delighted by her head. He often rubs his sister, while saying "Nice baby, nice baby," offers her a piece of his rice cracker, then goes about his business.